Land Cover Mapping of the National Park Service Northwest Alaska Management Area Using Landsat Multispectral and Thematic Mapper Satellite Data

By Carl J. Markon[1] and Sara Wesser[2]

Open-File Report 00-51

U.S. Department of the Interior
U.S. Geological Survey

[1]   Raytheon STX Corp., USGS/EROS Alaska Field Office, 4230 University Drive, Anchorage, AK. 99508-4664. E-mail: markon@usgs.gov. Work conducted under contract #1434-CR-97-40274

[2]   National Park Service, 2525 Gambell St., Anchorage, AK. 99503-2892

Land Cover Mapping of the National Park Service Northwest Alaska Management Area Using Landsat Multispectral Scanner and Thematic Mapper Satellite Data

ABSTRACT

A land cover map of the National Park Service northwest Alaska management area was produced using digitally processed Landsat data. These and other environmental data were incorporated into a geographic information system to provide baseline information about the nature and extent of resources present in this northwest Alaskan environment.

This report details the methodology, depicts vegetation profiles of the surrounding landscape, and describes the different vegetation types mapped. Portions of nine Landsat satellite (multispectral scanner and thematic mapper) scenes were used to produce a land cover map of the Cape Krusenstern National Monument and Noatak National Preserve and to update an existing land cover map of Kobuk Valley National Park Valley National Park. A Bayesian multivariate classifier was applied to the multispectral data sets, followed by the application of ancillary data (elevation, slope, aspect, soils, watersheds, and geology) to enhance the spectral separation of classes into more meaningful vegetation types. The resulting land cover map contains six major land cover categories (forest, shrub, herbaceous, sparse/barren, water, other) and 19 subclasses encompassing 7 million hectares. General narratives of the distribution of the subclasses throughout the project area are given along with vegetation profiles showing common relationships between topographic gradients and vegetation communities.

INTRODUCTION

In 1980, the Alaska National Interest Lands Conservation Act (Public Law 96-487) was enacted to provide and conserve additional federal public lands in Alaska. As part of the Act, the National Park Service (NPS) was instructed to manage and protect the natural and cultural resources in the area now encompassing the Cape Krusenstern National Monument, Noatak National Preserve, and Kobuk Valley National Park. To accomplish the overall management activities in this area, the NPS recognized a need for maps showing the location and extent of land cover. Originally, only broad or regional land cover classes (Kuchler 1966; Selkregg 1975) or use-specific land cover classifications (Soil Conservation Service 1984) existed for the newly formed management areas. Parts of Cape Krusenstern National Park and Kobuk Valley National Park were previously mapped by the NPS using Landsat thematic mapper (TM) data (Faeo, 1993; Wesser, 1994), but the northwest part of Cape Krusenstern National Park was not previously mapped and no medium-scale (1:100,000 to 1:250,000) land cover information existed for Noatak National Preserve.

After the previous Cape Krusenstern National Park and Kobuk Valley National Park mapping efforts were completed, more recent Landsat data (1985-92) became available for the entire northwest Alaska management areas. The NPS wanted to update existing maps using the new satellite data, as well as produce a new medium-scale land cover map of Noatak National Preserve and complete the unmapped areas of Cape Krusenstern National Park. As a result, the NPS established a cooperative program with the U.S. Geological Survey (USGS). This program followed other successful mapping efforts (Markon and Wesser, 1997).

The basis for the cooperative program was founded on previous work by the USGS in the northwest Alaska management area (Bering Land Bridge National Preserve, Markon and Wesser, 1997) and the USGS Multiresolution Land Characterization (MRLC) Program. The MRLC involves development of regional-scale land cover information from the analysis of remotely sensed data for support of management and research over Federal, State, and privately owned lands as well as national and international global change studies (Vogelmann and others, 1998, Vogelmann, Sohl, and Howard, 1998, Loveland and Shaw, 1996). The NPS was interested in the MRLC process as a possible additional tool to meet future management needs. The NPS also wanted to produce a seamless data base for the entire northwest Alaska management area (Bering Land Bridge National Preserve, Kobuk Valley National Park, Cape Krusenstern National Park, and Noatak National Preserve) using similar data types and methodology. This report summarizes the results of the land cover mapping project under the cooperative agreement through the MRLC program for the Kobuk Valley National Park, Cape Krusenstern National Park, and Noatak National Preserve areas.

PROJECT AREA

The three NPS management units are located in northwest Alaska (fig. 1). The Cape Krusenstern National Park and Noatak National Preserve areas lie entirely above the Arctic Circle, and the Kobuk Valley National Park is bisected by it. The northern border of Cape Krusenstern National Park lies just south of the Wulik River and is bordered on the west by the Chukchi Sea. To the south lies Kotzebue Sound, and the eastern border lies west of and parallels the Noatak river. The area consists primarily of moist and wet tundra in the lowlands and hills, with dryer tundra in the mountains. Large lagoons and wetland complexes are common along the western and southern coasts, and sand dunes are common along the southwest coast of Cape Krusenstern. Bedrock geology consists primarily of basic (limestone, dolomite, and marble) Devonian and Silurian rocks in the southern half and more acidic (sandstone, graywacke, and quartzite) Mississippian or Devonian rocks to the north (Biekman, 1980). Soils consist of loamy, near-level to rolling Histic Pergelic Cryaquepts (cold, wet soils with a thick organic layer and minimal weathering) in low coastal areas along the western and southern coasts to more gravelly Pergelic Cryaquepts or Pergelic Cryorthents (cold, wet soils with a thin organic layer and a minimal to small amount of leaching) in the central and northern lowlands and uplands (including low mountains; Rieger and others, 1979).

The Noatak National Preserve area is predominantly bordered on the north by the Delong Mountains, on the south by the Baird Mountains, on the west by the Noatak river (south of Kikmiksot Mountain), and on the east by the Schwatka Mountains; the bulk of the preserve lies within the Noatak River drainage. Conifers occupy much of the land in the lower wide valleys in the western part of the preserve, with high mountain peaks, wide, treeless, hilly valleys, and

3

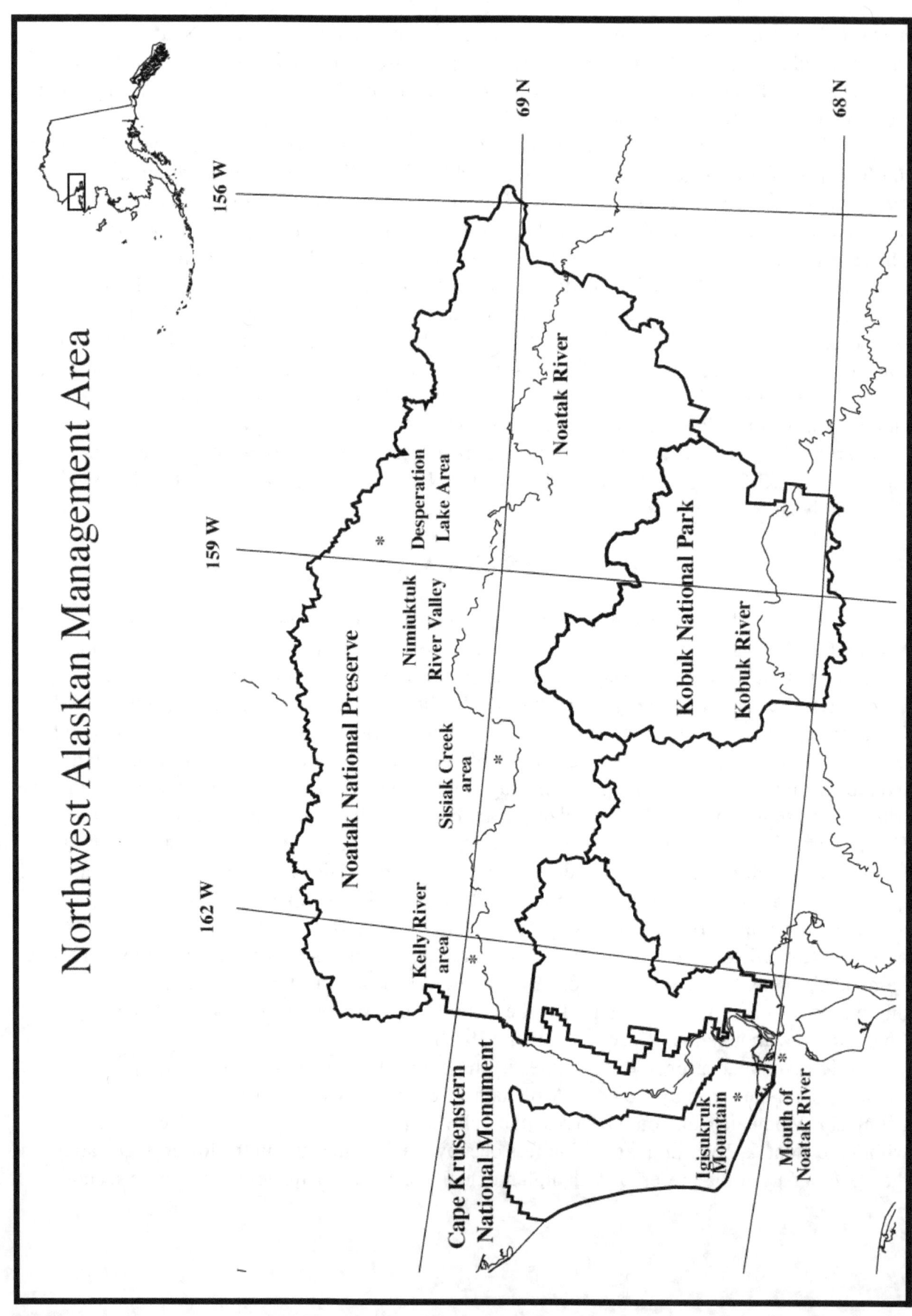

Figure 1. Location of National Park Service Northwest Alaska management areas.

plains in the east. Histic Pergelic Cryaquepts occur over much of the lower slopes along rivers, and Pergelic Cryaquolls (cold, wet, somewhat calcareous, more fertile soils with high organic carbon) and Typic Cryoborolls (slightly warmer fertile soils) occur on the upper slopes (Rieger and others, 1979). River flood plains and associated lower valley slopes in the northern part of the preserve are composed of moraines and modified moraines. Coarse- and fine-grained surficial deposits occur in the central part of the preserve, dominated by the Noatak River. To the east, roughly half of the preserve is composed of undifferentiated eolian, colluvial, fluvial, marine, and glacial deposits (Karlstrom and others, 1964).

Contiguous with the south and southeast boundary of the Noatak National Preserve is the Kobuk Valley National Park. The Kobuk Valley National Park is bounded roughly by the Baird Mountains to the north, the Kallarichuk Hills to the west, the Waring Mountains to the south, and the Jade Mountains to the east. The Kobuk Valley National Park River bisects the southern third of the park. The Great Kobuk Valley National Park and Little Kobuk Valley National Park Sand Dunes are prominent features south of the Kobuk Valley National Park River. Much of the park is covered by evergreen and deciduous forests, tall and low shrubland, and tundra. Surficial geology includes complex older coastal deposits of interstratified alluvial and marine sediments, which include glacial drift and small pockets of eolian silt up to 1.5 meters thick (Karlstrom and others, 1964). Soils are primarily composed of loamy, near-level to rolling Histic Pergelic Cryaquepts north of the Kobuk Valley National Park River and sandy Pergelic Cryorthods (cold, wet soils with slow leaching) and Pergelic Cryaquepts with dune intrusions to the south (Rieger and others, 1979).

Selkregg (1975) and Rieger and others (1979) report the following general vegetation types within the northwest Alaska management area: high brush, low brush bog and muskeg, moist tundra, alpine tundra and barren ground, and wet tundra. Upland and bottomland spruce forests and cottonwood-birch forests occur throughout the Kobuk Valley National Park and in the west and southwest parts of Noatak National Preserve, although the extent of deciduous forest in Noatak National Preserve is very small in comparison.

The growing season for the area as a whole is generally from mid-May to late August, with initial green-up beginning about mid-May in the southern part to mid-June in the northern part (Markon and others 1995). The three management areas cross three ecoregions (from north to south): Arctic Foothills, Brooks Range, and Interior Forested Lowlands and Uplands (Gallant and others, 1995).

METHODOLOGY

Data Base Design

Land cover mapping of the three management areas was performed in a raster digital data base format with all data georeferenced to an Albers Equal-Area Conic projection. Minimum data resolution for each picture element, or pixel, was 30 m by 30 m. A general schematic diagram of the data base development and mapping process is shown in figure 2.

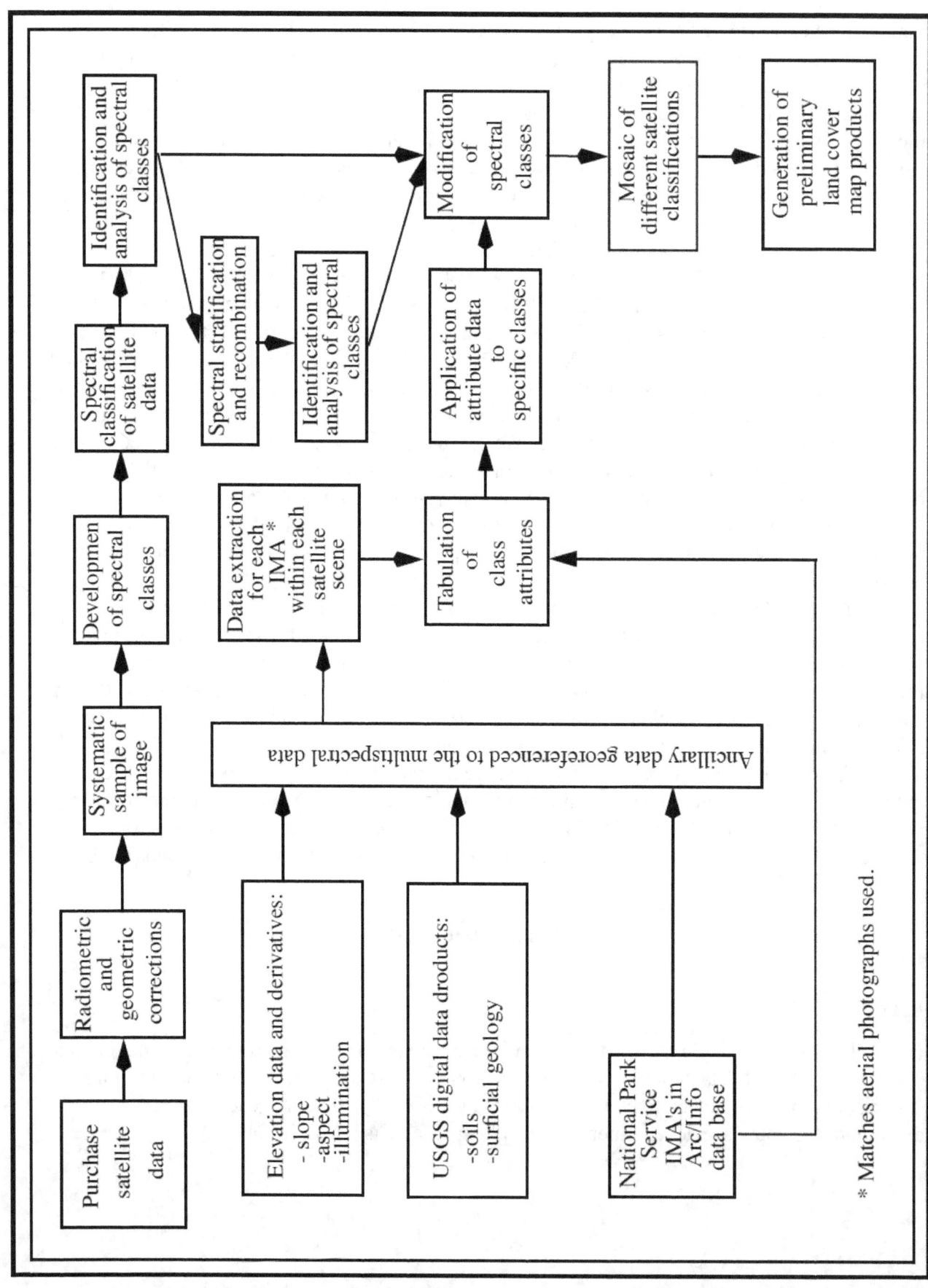

Figure 2. Schema for the National Park Service, northwest areas land cover mapping project.

Data Acquisition

Parts of nine Landsat scenes (table 1) were used to provide complete coverage of the three management areas and surrounding lands. Of the nine scenes, seven were Landsat TM mid-summer data sets and two were Landsat multispectral scanner (MSS) data sets obtained in late winter. Winter MSS data have proved to be efficient in separating conifer crown closure classes (for example, close, open, woodland; Fleming, 1988) and were used in the Noatak National Preserve and Kobuk Valley National Park areas.

Table 1. Landsat scene identification, path/row, and dates used for mapping the National Park Service northwest Alaska management areas

Sensor	Identification	Path	Row	Date
MSS	LM5080013008410390	80	13	April 12, 1984
MSS	LM5081012008411090	81	12	April 19, 1984
TM	LT 5078012008518710	78	12	July 06, 1985
TM	LT 5078013008520310	78	13	July 22, 1985
TM	LT 5079012008618110	79	12	June 30, 1986
TM	LT 4080012009221310	80	12	July 31, 1992
TM	LT 4080013009221310	80	13	July 31, 1992
TM	LT 5081012009022210	81	12	August 10, 1990
TM	LT 5081013009022210	81	13	August 10, 1990

Prior to digital analysis of the satellite data, NPS personnel selected 54 intensive mapping areas (IMA; Cape Krusenstern National Park - 16, Noatak National Preserve - 26, Kobuk Valley National Park - 12) and field visited them during a 4-year period (1988-91). These sample areas, which represent land cover types within the project area, correspond to 1:60,000-scale color-infrared aerial photographs (circa 1979-85), and they were used as training blocks, as described by Fleming (1975, 1988), Talbot and others (1986), and Wesser (1994). On each sample area photograph, photointerpreted polygons were subjectively drawn around what appeared to be homogeneous plant communities. This resulted in a total of 657 polygons (Cape Krusenstern National Park - 119, Noatak National Preserve - 380, KOVA - 158). A ground survey of each polygon determined vegetation cover, structure, and general species composition information using procedures similar to those described by Talbot and Markon (1988) and Faeo (1993).

Preprocessing

Each Landsat scene was reviewed to ensure adequate project area coverage and confirm the presence and location of clouds or bad data. The data used for this project were free of line drops and cloud cover was minimal. Satellite scenes from the same path and date were mosaicked and treated as a single data set during the initial image analysis; the other scenes were analyzed individually.

Georeferencing of each Landsat scene was done at the EROS Data Center in Sioux Falls,

S. Dak. The process was started by selecting recognizable points collocated on the Landsat scenes and USGS 1:63,360-scale topographic maps. These points were used to define a second-order, least squares polynomial transformation relating coordinates in an Albers Equal-Area Conic projection to the row and column locations within each scene. Displacement effects caused by differences in terrain elevation also were addressed. Mean residual errors associated with the second-order transformation resulted in a registration accuracy within +/- 1.0 pixel. Dimensions and georeferenced coordinates for the project area section are shown in table 2.

Ancillary digital data obtained for the project area included 1:250,000-scale digital elevation data (and the derivatives, slope, aspect, and illumination), 1:1,000,000-scale soils, 1:2,500,000-scale bedrock geology, and 1:250,000-scale watersheds. The soils, geology, and watershed data sets were digitized and converted to georeferenced raster formats coregistered to the raster Landsat data. Although these data are at much coarser resolutions than the Landsat TM data, they were the best ancillary information available. In addition to these data, the NPS supplied a digitized preserve boundary and other point and polygon data containing vegetation information from the IMA field studies.

Table 2. Registration parameters used for the National Park Service northwest Alaska management area land cover mapping project

---

Number of Lines: 9,936   **Number of Samples:**   15,244
                                    Number of Bands: 1

Data type: Byte   **Projection Code:** (3) Albers Equal-Area Conic

Zone Code: 62   **Semimajor Axis:** 6.3782064E+06
                                    Semiminor Axis: 6.76865799972911E-03

Latitude of first standard parallel: 5.50000+07
Latitude of second standard parallel: 6.50000+07
Longitude of the central meridian: -1.54000+08
Latitude of projection origin: 5.00000+07

Corner Coordinates:
    Upper Left Corner :   2.129820E+06-4.77540E+05
    Upper Right Corner :   2.129820E+06-2.02500E+04
    Lower Left corner :   1.831770E+06-4.77540E+05
    Lower Right corner :   1.831770E+06-2.02500E+04

Pixel Size: 30 X 30
Pixel Units: meters
Pixel Increment: 1 row by 1 column

Digital elevation data were originally acquired from the Defense Mapping Agency (DMA). The DMA generated the data by digitizing hypsographic features (contour lines, ridge lines, lake boundaries, and point data) from USGS map series (1:63,360 through 1:250,000 scale) and converting them to rectangular grid values with a 3-arc-second by 3-arc-second interval. Slope, aspect, and illumination were computed from the digital elevation data (Ailts and others, 1990). Slope was expressed as percentage slope (that is, units of rise per 100 units of run). Aspect values ranged from 0 to 360 (1-degree increments) in a clockwise direction from true north and were reassigned to values ranging from 0 to 180 (2-degree increments) for conversion to 8- bit data. Illumination was based on the Sun's elevation and azimuth at the time each Landsat scene was acquired. The computed illumination data resulted in values from 0 to 255, indicating a relative amount of radiance to the ground surface; low values indicated shadows and high values indicated sunny slopes.

Development of Spectral Statistics and Image Classification

Statistics used to generate the preliminary classification were derived individually for each summer satellite scene using a two-step, unsupervised and partially supervised classification process (Swain and Davis, 1978). The first step involved sampling the spectral variability in the satellite scene by extracting every 10th row and column from bands 1 - 5 and 7. The sample output was then used to produce 40 to 50 (number subjectively predetermined) discrete spectral clusters on the basis of brightness value of each pixel in each band using an isodata algorithm. Each cluster was defined in terms of descriptive statistics (means, standard deviations, covariance matrices between bands) for all bands (Swain and Davis, 1978). Redundant or overlapping statistics in the initial statistical data set were manually removed or combined, on the basis of descriptive statistics, to form a final set of cluster statistics that provided an independent estimate of the spectral characteristics of each scene being analyzed. Landsat band 6, the thermal band, was not used because of its lower pixel resolution (120 m) and its poor information content in relation to vegetation type and condition.

A Bayesian maximum likelihood classification algorithm (Swain and Davis, 1978) was used to apply the cluster statistics to the entire Landsat scene. The algorithm used a complex mathematical decision rule for evaluating the pixel brightness values compared to the descriptive statistic values obtained for each cluster. Each pixel was then assigned to one of the spectral clusters on the probability that the pixel belonged to the spectral class of that cluster. The result was a spectral classification where each pixel fell into a spectral class.

The spectrally classified satellite scene was then evaluated and each class assigned to a land cover class name on the basis of interpreted color-infrared aerial photographs and field data descriptions. Spectral class inconsistencies within and between geographical areas were noted for possible refinement.

The second step in the classification process occurred after the class labeling described above. A spectral class may include two different vegetation types that are spectrally distinct but not sampled sufficiently during the initial sample to allow for identification of some classes (for example, linear habitats falling between sample units). If these areas were known to exist in a specific class, spectral stratification was used (Ailts and others, 1990). The problem class (from the preliminary classified image) was used as a pattern to extract multispectral information from the original satellite image (bands 1-5 and 7). This produced a small, multispectral image containing spectral qualities for only that class. The isodata algorithm was then used on this smaller image to produce two to four new spectral clusters. These new clusters were then incorporated into the original classification and labeled as described above.

Postclassification Refinement Using Ancillary Data

Correct identifications of land cover types from preliminary classifications are often low because of similar spectral response from (1) the presence of similar vegetation type, (2) the effects of shadow and water on the overall reflectance of the vegetation, and (3) subtle changes in vegetation type owing to elevation, slope, or aspect. To improve classification accuracy, ancillary data were applied to distinguish classes that were known to be misclassified. For example, slope and aspect were used to separate shadow from water, and elevation and aspect were used to separate lowland shrub types from upland shrub types. The winter Landsat MSS data were used to differentiate three conifer crown closure classes and to separate closed conifer from other land cover types. Also, the winter MSS data were used to separate some closed conifer types that were spectrally similar to water and some tall shrub types with tall dead stems. This was accomplished by viewing band 4 of the winter MSS data on a display screen and recording the digital numbers corresponding to features shown on aerial photographs and described in field data. For example, digital numbers from 0 to 46 were found to represent closed conifer, 47 to 80 open conifer, and 81 to 89 conifer woodland. These ranges of values were then renumbered to one, two, and three, respectively, and made into a mask. The mask was then matched with areas mapped as conifers in the original spectral data. Those conifer classes that corresponded to one on the mask (digital values of 0 to 46) were then identified as closed conifer; this was repeated for those areas with mask values of two and three.

Digital and Hard-Copy Products

Final digital products for the three management areas include; original georeferenced Landsat TM and MSS images, land cover, elevation, slope, aspect, and preserve or park boundary. All digital data were stored on transferable media (CD-ROM, tape, and ftp site). Color hard-copy maps of the land cover were produced at a scale of 1:500,000.

Assessment of Final Land Cover Map

A subjective assessment of the land cover map was made using a random 10-percent sample of the polygons used during the ground sampling and classification process. For each polygon selected we recorded the land cover type previously identified by the field crew, along with the types and quantity of land cover pixels falling in the polygon from the final map. Field-based vegetation descriptions were used to assign relative levels of classification uncertainty, or "fuzzy labels" (table 3; also see Gopal and Woodcock, 1994), to each land cover class occurring in each polygon. For example, a polygon identified as open low shrub-birch/ericaceous in the field may have the following combination of classes associated with it: (1) 10 pixels of open low shrub - birch/ericaceous, (2) 5 pixels of open low and dwarf shrub tussock tundra, (3) 1 pixel of clear water, and (4) 1 pixel of wet herbaceous, for a total of 17 pixels. Fuzzy labels given to each of these could be 5, 4, 1, and 1, respectively. Because each polygon often contains two or more

10

land cover classes, the normal set of outputs from a fuzzy logic accuracy assessment was not produced (Gopal and Woodcock, 1994; Markon and Wesser, 1997; Muller and others, 1998). Instead, two tables were produced, one that showed the total number of pixels by fuzzy label, and the other summing the number of pixels occurring in each land cover class by fuzzy label (similar to the Match/Mismatch table as reported by Gopal and Woodcock).

Table 3. Fuzzy label values and descriptions used in assessing land cover types

Fuzzy Label	Description
1	Absolutely wrong. Land cover type has no relationship to actual vegetation type.
2	Wrong. There is very little relationship between the land cover type and the vegetation type described.
3	Somewhat correct. Land cover type matches some of the attributes of actual vegetation. Should be used with caution depending on application of map.
4	Mostly correct. Land cover type could be used for most applications (difference probably due to subject cut points for height or percentage cover of a plant type).
5	Absolutely correct. Land cover exactly matches vegetation description.

RESULTS

Land cover Map

The land cover mapping process for the three management areas resulted in six major land cover categories (forest, shrub, herbaceous, sparse/barren, water, other), which were further separated into 19 classes (table 4). Class values were numbered to maintain consistency with other mapping projects. A narrative of each class is found in appendix A, along with class codes corresponding to hierarchical vegetation classification by Viereck and others (1992); a color hard-copy example of the final land cover map is found in the back of a limited number of copies of this report. Class summaries below are described first for the entire project and then for each management unit.

Project Area

For the entire project area (table 5), open low and dwarf shrub tussock tundra was the largest class, covering a little more than 1.1 million hectares, or 16 percent. The second largest class was open low shrub-birch/ericaceous, with 1.07 million hectares (15 percent), closely followed by clear water (a little less than 931,00 hectares, or 13 percent). Much of the water class (approximately 82 percent) occurs in the ocean, and a very small amount occurs in mountainous areas (owing to shadow effects), which could not be removed with elevation data or its derivatives, slope and aspect. The fourth largest class was open low shrub-alder/willow, with

11

about 661,000 hectares, followed by moist or dry herbaceous with over 516,000 hectares. It should be noted that these two classes may be confused if visited in the field because variations in the amount of graminoids present may be high in the tussock type.

Table 4. Land cover classes and class values used for the National Park Service's northwest Alaska management areas land cover map

Major Category	Subclass	Class Value
Forest	Closed needleleaf forest	1
	Open needleleaf forest	2
	Needleleaf woodland	3
Shrub	Tall open and closed alder/willow	8
	Closed low shrub - alder/willow	9
	Closed low shrub - birch/ericaceous	10
	Open low shrub - alder/willow	11
	Open low shrub - birch/ericacious	12
	Open low and dwarf shrub tussock tundra	13
	Dwarf shrub tundra/dwarf shrub peatland	14
	Open dwarf shrub - talus/lichen	17
Herbaceous	Moist or dry herbaceous	19
	Wet herbaceous	20
Sparse/barren	Sparsely vegetated	22
	Barren	23
	Snow/Ice/Cloud	24
Water	Clear water	25
	Turbid water	26
Other	Shadow	27

Table 5. Hectare summaries for each class for the entire National Park Service northwest Alaska management area and surrounding lands (LCC = land cover class number, Npixels = number of pixels)

LCC	Class Description	Npixels	Hectares	
1	Closed needleleaf forest	1,222,932	110,064	1.57%
2	Open needleleaf forest	2,974,111	267,670	3.81%
3	Needleleaf woodland	2,438,090	219,428	3.13%
8	Tall open and closed alder/willow	1,702,662	153,240	2.18%
9	Closed low shrub-alder/willow	2,992,922	269,363	3.84%
10	Closed low shrub-birch/ericaceous	1,175,742	105,817	1.51%
11	Open low shrub-alder/willow	7,344,120	660,971	9.42%
12	Open low shrub-birch/ericaceous	11,937,475	1,074,373	15.31%
13	Open low and dwarf shrub tussock tundra	12,497,862	1,124,808	16.03%
14	Dwarf shrub tundra/dwarf shrub peatland	4,755,835	428,025	6.10%
17	Open dwarf shrub-talus/lichen	2,608,643	234,778	3.35%
19	Moist or dry herbaceous	5,740,292	516,626	7.36%
20	Wet herbaceous	1,194,115	107,470	1.53%
22	Sparsely vegetated	3,033,807	273,043	3.89%
23	Barren	4,896,944	440,725	6.28%
24	Snow/ice/cloud	108,720	9,785	0.14%
25	Clear water	10,341,271	930,714	13.26%
26	Turbid water	226,391	20,375	0.29%
27	Shadow	773,478	69,613	0.99%
	Total	77,965,412	7,016,887	

The barren class makes up over 440,000 hectares (over 6 percent) of the final map, occurring primarily in the De Long, Baird, Waring, and Schwatka Mountains, and the Mulgrave and Igichuk Hills. The sparsely vegetated class covered approximately one-half of the area (230,000 hectares).

The dwarf shrub tundra/dwarf shrub peatland was found on slightly more than 428,000 hectares (roughly 6 percent). This class may be underrepresented throughout the project area because of complex species mixing in this vegetation type. Open alder/willow communities occur throughout the area, but varying amounts of graminoid, dwarf birch, and ericaceous shrubs are often present in the understory, making it difficult to separate them from the open low shrub - dwarf birch/ericaceous shrub class.

Forests occur throughout the central and eastern parts of the project area. Open needleleaf is the most extensive, with over 267,000 hectares (4 percent), followed by needleleaf woodland, with 219,000 hectares (or 3 percent). Closed needleleaf forest was the smallest forested class, with 110,00 hectares (2 percent). Although open mixed forest is found in the Kobuk Valley National Park area, it could not be adequately distinguished from other vegetation classes.

Other prominent classes that have less than 5 percent coverage of the project area include closed low shrub-alder/willow, with a little more than 269,000 hectares, open dwarf shrub-talus lichen, with close to 235,000 hectares, and moist or dry herbaceous, with about 107,000 hectares.

13

Cape Krusenstern National Monument

Within the Cape Krusenstern National Monument (table 6), four vegetation classes cover close to 70 percent of the area. Open low shrub-birch/ericaceous occupied the largest area, with almost 85,000 hectares (32 percent), followed by open low and dwarf shrub tussock tundra, with about 55,000 hectares (20 percent). These two types were well distributed throughout the

Table 6. Hectare summaries for each class for Cape Krusenstern National Preserve (LCC = land cover class number, Npixels = number of pixels)

LCC	Class Description	Npixels	Hectares	
1	Closed needleleaf forest	696	63	0.02%
2	Open needleleaf forest	3,746	337	0.13%
3	Needleleaf woodland	1,506	136	0.05%
8	Tall open and closed alder/willow	127,179	11,446	4.28%
9	Closed low shrub-alder/willow	93,220	8,390	3.14%
10	Closed low shrub-birch/ericaceous	165,724	14,915	5.58%
11	Open low shrub-alder/willow	94,069	8,466	3.17%
12	Open low shrub-birch/ericaceous	943,655	84,929	31.77%
13	Open low and dwarf shrub tussock tundra	607,519	54,677	20.46%
14	Dwarf shrub tundra/dwarf shrub peatland	113,197	10,188	3.81%
17	Open dwarf shrub-talus/lichen	74,662	6,720	2.51%
19	Moist or dry herbaceous	324,377	29,194	10.92%
20	Wet herbaceous	91,155	8,204	3.07%
22	Sparsely vegetated	41,414	3,727	1.39%
23	Barren	78,537	7,068	2.64%
24	Snow/ice/cloud	0	0	0.00%
25	Clear water	202,312	18,208	6.81%
26	Turbid water	6,386	575	0.22%
27	Shadow	564	51	0.02%
	Total	2,969,918	267,293	

monument, occurring on low rolling hills and lower mountain slopes. Moist or dry herbaceous covered a little over 29,000 hectares (11 percent) and was most prevalent near the coast in lowland areas, especially in the northern part of the monument. Clear water was the fourth largest class mapped (7 percent). Closed low shrub-birch/ericaceous was fairly common in the region, with almost 15,000 hectares (6 percent), followed by tall open and closed alder/willow (about 11,500 hectares), occurring primarily in drainages and water tracks on upper slopes.

Dwarf shrub tundra/dwarf shrub peatland occurred on a little more than 10,000 hectares (just under 4 percent). Open low shrub-alder/willow occurred on roughly 8,500 hectares (3 percent), primarily along water courses and lower hill slopes, although it also fringed conifer types on middle and upper slopes.

Wet herbaceous sites were less prominent in the monument, covering about 8,200 hectares (3 percent) and occurring in low areas, especially within and near the coastal lagoons. It should be noted that both the wet herbaceous and moist or dry herbaceous types also may occur in upper mountain valleys in the north.

All other classes covered less than 3 percent of the area.

14

Noatak National Preserve management area

The Noatak National Preserve has both preserve and wilderness designations. Although table 7 provides total hectares by land cover class for both, the following summarizes the land cover types over the entire management area.

Four land cover classes occupied more than 50 percent of the land area (1.62 million hectares) of the Noatak National Preserve. Open low shrub-dwarf shrub tussock tundra covered the largest area (20 percent), being a prominent cover type on the many rolling hills and lower mountain slopes. Associated with this class and occurring on the same type of terrain was open low shrub- birch/ericaceous covering 17 percent. Vegetatively, these two types are very similar, the main difference being the amount of tussock-forming graminoid present (that is, *Carex bigelowii* or *Eriophorum vaginatum*). Transitions between the two are often subtle and difficult to map. The third largest class was open low shrub- alder/willow (14 percent). This class was found primarily on mid-slopes of hills and mountains with low ericaceous shrub types occurring both below and above. In some areas, this class had an understory dominated by dwarf birch and ericaceous plants, which in some areas may be mapped as an open low shrub-dwarf birch/ericaceous type.

The fourth class was moist or dry herbaceous (11 percent). In many cases, this class was difficult to separate from wet herbaceous, which may be the reason for such low coverage (less than 1 percent). These two types are often difficult to separate, both *in situ* and by remote sensing. Local, short-term climate conditions may change the appearance of a moist herbaceous site to that of a wet herbaceous site simply by the amount and duration of rainfall occurring shortly before satellite images were obtained or the field crew visited the site.

The fifth largest class mapped in the area was barren, with close to 216,000 hectares (9 percent), occurring primarily in the mountains but also found in the lower reaches of the Noatak River. Dwarf shrub tundra/dwarf shrub peatland was somewhat common throughout the preserve with about 209,000 hectares (8 percent), especially in the east, where it occurred on mountain slopes, lower valley reaches, and bottomlands.

Sparsely vegetated and open dwarf shrub- talus/lichen were present, but not in large amounts (about 5 percent of the total area for both). Both of these types commonly occur in transition areas between more densely vegetated areas on lower slopes and barren areas on upper slopes.

Closed low shrub-alder/willow is fairly common throughout the preserve, although in small amounts (less than 3 percent), occurring primarily in drainages along stream and river shorelines, and in larger floodplains. It can often be mapped incorrectly as tall open and closed alder/willow (which covered about 2 percent of the area) because the only prominent separation is height (greater than 1.5 m). In the lower Noatak River area, either of these classes also may contain aspen (*Populus tremuloides*) and cottonwood (*Populus balsamifera*).

Kobuk Valley National Park

Among the most prominent differences between the Kobuk Valley National Park and the other two management areas are the extensive forests and the presence of active sand dunes. Open needleleaf forest occupies a little less than 88,00 hectares (table 8), closely followed by

Table 7. Hectare summaries for each class for the Noatak National Monument (LCC = land cover class number, Npixels = number of pixels)

LCC	Class Description	Preserve			Wilderness			Total		
		Npixels	Hectares	%	Npixels	Hectares	%	Npixels	Hectares	%
1	Closed needleleaf forest	37,717	3,395	0.14	22,892	2,060	0.67	60,609	5,455	0.21
2	Open needleleaf forest	88,733	7,986	0.34	79,127	7,121	2.32	167,860	15,107	0.57
3	Needleleaf woodland	136,161	12,254	0.52	67,332	6,060	1.97	203,493	18,314	0.69
8	Tall open and closed alder/willow	436,140	39,253	1.67	55,002	4,950	1.61	491,142	44,203	1.66
9	Closed low shrub-alder/willow	759,397	68,346	2.91	38,193	3,437	1.12	797,590	71,783	2.70
10	Closed low shrub-birch/ericaceous	279,563	25,161	1.07	72,267	6,504	2.12	351,830	31,665	1.19
11	Open low shrub-alder/willow	3,807,229	342,651	14.57	452,654	40,739	13.26	4,259,883	383,389	14.42
12	Open low shrub-birch/ericaceous	4,337,606	390,385	16.60	755,765	68,019	22.15	5,093,371	458,403	17.24
13	Open low and dwarf shrub tussock tundra	5,281,952	475,376	20.22	585,728	52,716	17.16	5,867,680	528,091	19.87
14	Dwarf shrub tundra/dwarf shrub peatland	2,122,341	191,011	8.12	206,188	18,557	6.04	2,328,529	209,568	7.88
17	Open dwarf shrub-talus/lichen	1,328,565	119,571	5.09	107,245	9,652	3.14	1,435,810	129,223	4.86
19	Moist or dry herbaceous	2,857,120	257,141	10.94	285,667	25,710	8.37	3,142,787	282,851	10.64
20	Wet herbaceous	179,535	16,158	0.69	55,924	5,033	1.64	235,459	21,191	0.80
22	Sparsely vegetated	1,416,502	127,485	5.42	190,624	17,156	5.59	1,607,126	144,641	5.44
23	Barren	2,399,858	215,987	9.19	363,813	32,743	10.66	2,763,671	248,730	9.36
24	Snow/ice/cloud	56,281	5,065	0.22				56,281	5,065	0.19
25	Clear water	265,499	23,895	1.02	47,963	4,317	1.41	313,462	28,212	1.06
26	Turbid water	158,779	14,290	0.61	1,572	141	0.05	160,351	14,432	0.54
27	Shadow	174,138	15,672	0.67	24,767	2,229	0.73	198,905	17,901	0.67
	Total	26,123,116	2,351,080		3,412,723	307,145		29,535,839	2,658,226	

Table 8. Hectare summaries for each class for the Kobuk National Park (LCC = land cover class number, Npixels = number of pixels)

LCC	Class Description	Npixels	Hectares	%
1	Closed needleleaf forest	296,623	26,696	3.77
2	Open needleleaf forest	977,484	87,974	12.44
3	Needleleaf woodland	947,304	85,257	12.05
8	Tall open and closed alder/willow	221,394	19,925	2.82
9	Closed low shrub-alder/willow	762,473	68,623	9.70
10	Closed low shrub-birch/ericaceous	206,281	18,565	2.63
11	Open low shrub-alder/willow	456,073	41,047	5.80
12	Open low shrub-birch/ericaceous	954,588	85,913	12.15
13	Open low and dwarf shrub tussock tundra	1,333,111	119,980	16.96
14	Dwarf shrub tundra/dwarf shrub peatland	447,772	40,299	5.70
17	Open dwarf shrub-talus/lichen	134,591	12,113	1.71
19	Moist or dry herbaceous	134,234	12,081	1.71
20	Wet herbaceous	10,828	975	0.14
22	Sparsely vegetated	202,337	18,210	2.57
23	Barren	362,087	32,588	4.61
24	Snow/ice/cloud	13	1	0.00
25	Clear water	262,282	23,605	3.34
26	Turbid water	1,369	123	0.02
27	Shadow	147,347	13,261	1.88
	Total	7,858,191	707,237	

needleleaf woodland, with a little more than 85,000 hectares. Small amounts of closed needleleaf forest were mapped (less than 28,000 hectares), occurring along and within the Kobuk River floodplain. The largest class mapped was open low and dwarf shrub tussock tundra, with a little less than 120,000 hectares (17 percent); it is ubiquitous throughout the Park. Closed low shrub-alder/willow was less common, covering more than 68,000 hectares (10 percent), occurring along all stream and river courses, most low to middle slopes of mountains, and high hills, and often revegetating burned forest areas. Open low shrub-alder willow occupied similar sites, with about 41,000 hectares (6 percent). Of the alder/willow types, tall open and closed alder/willow was the least prominent, with just under 20,000 hectares (3 percent). As with the open class, this type also occurred on mid-mountain slopes and along water courses.

Dwarf shrub tundra/dwarf shrub peatland was the seventh largest class mapped, with a little more than 40,000 hectares (6 percent), occurring primarily on upper slopes in the northern part of the park. Open low shrub-birch/ericaceous covered about one-half as much area, less than 19,000 hectares (3 percent), occurring primarily in the Kobuk River valley.

Barren areas covered over 32,000 hectares (5 percent), owing to the extensive mountains in the northern half of the park.

Phytogeographic patterns

Vegetation patterns across the landscape are based on a number of physiographic, edaphic, climatic, and topographic processes. A series of vegetation profiles and site descriptions based primarily on topographic characteristics were obtained for Cape

Krusenstern National Park and Noatak National Preserve areas during brief helicopter overflights and a limited number of landings in 1995, 1996, and 1997. Because of constraints in flight time and landing restrictions, only general representations of the many and varied conditions for the two management areas are given; similar overflights were not performed for Kobuk Valley National Park. In general, the following descriptions begin at the Noatak River delta, proceed north through the Cape Krusenstern National Park and western Noatak National Preserve, northward to the Kelly River, and then eastward through the Noatak River watershed and tributaries culminating in the Cutler River drainage.

Just north of the village of Kotzebue, the Noatak River forms a small delta as it empties into Kotzebue Sound. On the east side of the delta, mud flats quickly transition from mud to graminoid to open shrub types, followed by open needleleaf forest and woodland (primarily of *Picea glauca*). The west side of the delta is somewhat different in that there are much fewer trees and shrubs, possibly indicating a younger or more active flood plain.

To the north, as the landscape rises up out of the active floodplain and delta area into Cape Krusenstern National Park, conifers are more prevalent, forming small stands of forests, especially on the upper hillslopes. In the lower rolling hills, low shrub-graminoid tussock tundra is prominent on all slopes and aspects, with open and closed alder (*Alnus* spp.) or willow (*Salix* spp.) thickets in drainages and around lake and pond ridges. Alder also is found on the lower and upper slopes of mountains, with other types of communities on the mid-slopes. A common topographic sequence (fig. 3) is alder on the toe slope, forming a transition zone between tussock tundra below and needleleaf forest above, extending through the needleleaf forest and beyond the treeline to the upper slope. Above this, the alder thins out into low and dwarf shrub communities (*Betula nana*, *Cassiope tetragona*, *Dryas* spp., and *Arctostaphylos rubra*, to name a few), occurring with various graminoids and forbs. The upper slope finally culminates with a lichen-barren talus community and a few scattered dwarf and prostrate shrubs.

In the central part of Cape Krusenstern National Park is a small valley situated between the Igichuk Hills to the south and the Mulgrave Hills to the north; it is the site of a westward lobe of a middle Pleistocene glacier that covered the Noatak valley (Coulter and others, 1965). This area consists of rolling hills less than 200 meters high, with small ponds and lakes in the east and central part and numerous small wetlands to the west. Open low ericaceous shrubs (for example, *Vaccinium uliginosum*, *V. vitis-idaea*, *Ledum palustre*, *Empetrum nigrum*) dominate the hills along with areas of low shrub-graminoid tussock tundra. Bordering small streams, ponds, and lake shorelines are open tall and low willow, often with an ericaceous shrub understory.

Between the lower Noatak Canyon and Kelly River is a wide valley that has broad, low rolling hills less than 100 m high, gently sloping toward the Noatak River with numerous lakes, ponds, and wetlands. In this area, three different types of shrub communities occur, depending on local hydrology. In areas of moderate to swift flowing water away from the main active Noatak River floodplain, found in stream channels or in areas of sheet wash, low willow dominates. In other areas, where the water is slow moving or is found in small pockets owing to a shallow thaw layer, dwarf birch and other ericaceous shrubs dominate. In areas near the active floodplain of the Noatak River, where the substrate is generally warmer

18

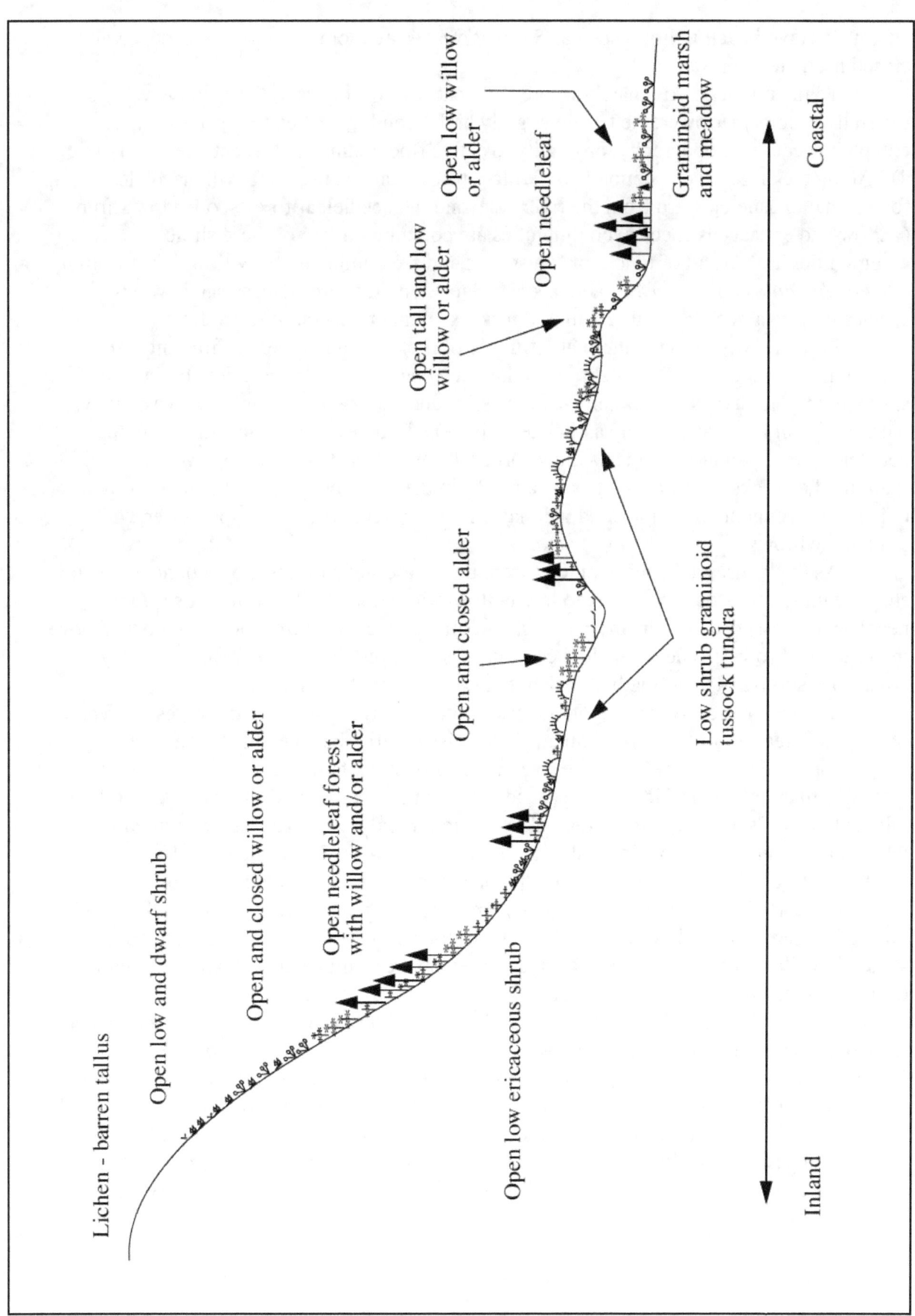

Figure 3. Typical vegetation profile from mouth of Noatak River to Igisukruk Mountain in southeast Cape Krusenstern National Monument.

and more gravelly, tall willows such as *Salix alaxensis* are more common, as are open and closed needleleaf forests.

To the north, approximately where the Noatak River bends to the east, the valleys generally become narrower, the terrain slightly higher, and the vegetation patterns more complex because of topography, proximity to active floodplains, and recent fire history (fig. 4). Along the larger rivers, cottonwood-willow forests can occur, along with needleleaf forests that expand outward from the river. Beyond the needleleaf forests, open low shrub (willow and ericaceous species) communities are common. Some of these shrub communities are a result of tundra or forest fires and are dominated by willows, dwarf birch (*Betula glandulosa, B. nana*), and ericaceous plants. In other areas, these same woody species may be associated with graminoid tussocks but not necessarily with fires.

Further away from the thermal influence of the river, a number of different plant communities may occur. Dwarf shrub peatland may be found in low shallow basins with low shrub graminoid tussock communities on the surrounding low, rolling hills. Occasionally, there are small knolls commonly associated with water bodies and streams in which open needleleaf forests or closed alder/willow shrubs occur. These knolls often have low shrub graminoid tussocks on the opposite side away from the water body. Small depressions are numerous throughout the valley and will have moist or wet herbaceous types, often with scattered willows.

As the landscape begins a quick ascent up the toe slope of a nearby mountain, the low shrub graminoid tussocks give way to low willow-ericaceous shrub communities. Open needleleaf forests occur again about mid-slope, often associated with alder or willow. Above the needleleaf forests, alder or willow communities are present and eventually give way to ericaceous shrub and then finally to lichen talus at the mountain crest.

The next major river valley to the east is the Kugururok River. An interesting feature of the lower reaches of this river drainage is the dissimilarity between the east and west valley slopes. Distances between the river and nearby mountain peaks are shorter on the west side than on the east side. The east side is primarily represented by broad, low rolling hills with dwarf shrub- graminoid tussock or by graminoid-dominated tussock tundra with tall and low stands of willow in small drainages. On the west side, closed stands of needleleaf forest are common in the floodplain and may continue up to mid-slope. Low shrubs and dwarf shrub-graminoid tussock communities occur in the surrounding hills and open tundra areas as well as the lower mountain slopes. As with the east side, tall and low stands of willow occur in smaller drainages. In some areas, moist graminoid communities occur above the treeline and lichen talus is common on upper slopes.

Upriver from the Kugururok is the Kaluktavik River. This relatively small drainage is notable in that needleleaf forests are absent; however, large groves of cottonwood (*Populus balsamifera*) are present. Since these stands are a few kilometers upstream from the river's confluence with the Noatak River, it is not known if the seed source was brought in by wind or by animal-borne vectors, or if the stands are relics from larger forests that may have been there in the past (Bob Gall, NPS, oral communication). Small cottonwood groves (10-30 trees) also can be found along the Noatak River, up to and including its confluence with the Nimiuktuk River.

20

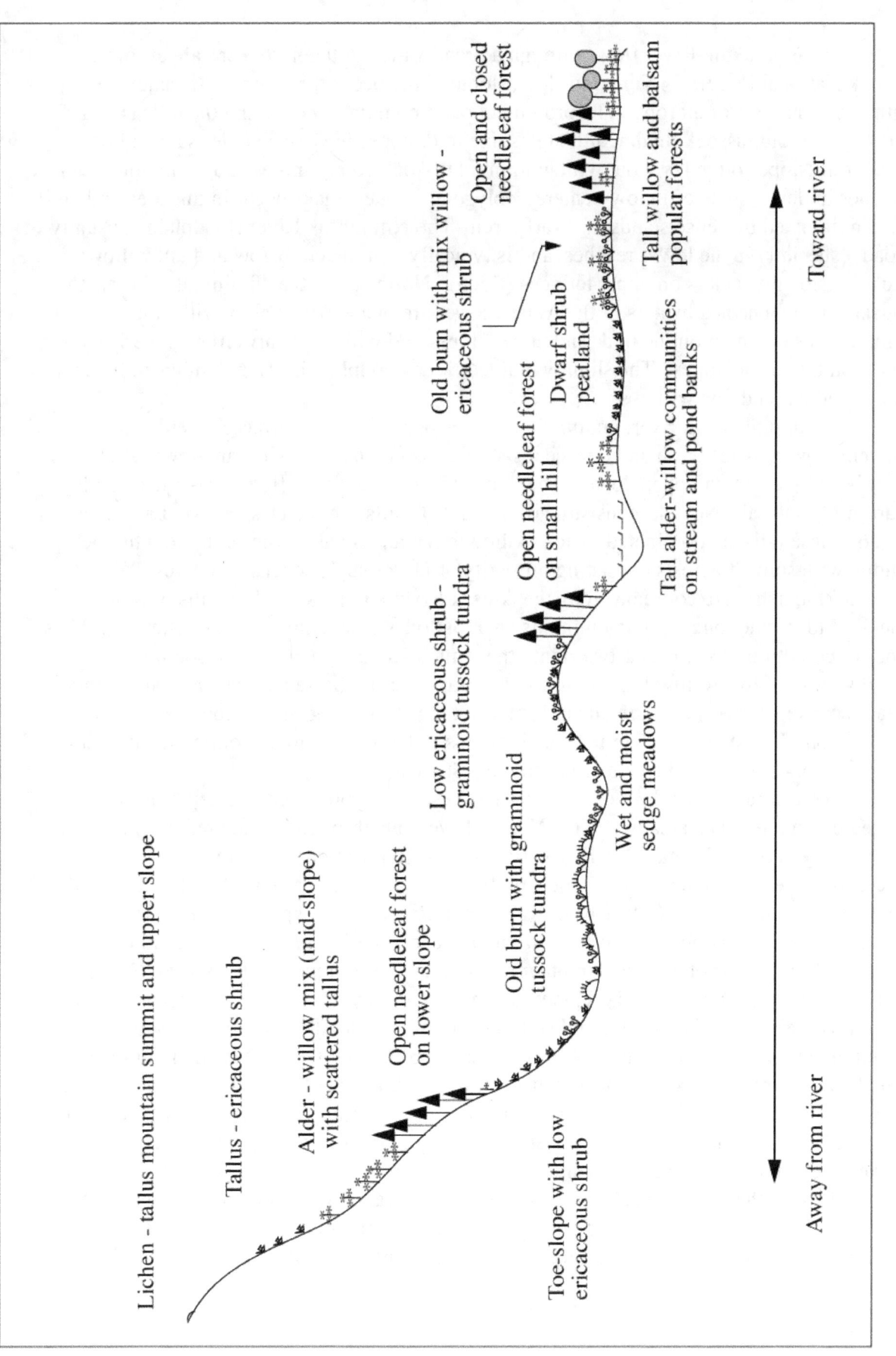

Figure 4. Vegetation profile of the Kelly River area.

The Nimiuktuk River flows through a broad valley in the north central part of the Noatak National Preserve. Numerous low, sloping hills occur throughout the valley, along with occasional rock outcrops. The prominent plant community covering the hills is dwarf shrub-graminoid tussock tundra, although some mid-slopes have open alder stands. Lower parts of hillslopes often level out with graminoid tussock communities and graminoid marshes in depressions or in low-centered polygons. Water tracks occur in this area and are often dominated by dense stands of dwarf birch. The Nimiuktuk River floodplain is usually broad, especially in the lower reaches, and is typically dominated by low and tall willows and, occasionally, alders on upper terraces (fig. 5). Northeast of the Nimiuktuk River is the Anisak River. The headwaters of the Anisak River are in a narrow valley with alder communities common on the mid- and upper-slopes and willow, dwarf birch, and ericaceous plants on the lower slopes. The slightly braided river floodplain is often dominated by open and closed tall and low willows.

Continuing down river, graminoid marshes occur on level terraces on either side of the valley, with dwarf birch and ericaceous shrubs occupying drier sites and lower slopes; alder is still present on upper slopes. The Anisak River eventually flows into a wide valley (part of glacial Lake Noatak) consisting of broad, low hills. In the Desperation Lake area (fig. 6), these hills are dominated by low willow/birch and dwarf shrub-graminoid tussock tundra, with some hillcrests consisting primarily of *Dryas* spp., lichens, and talus. Wet graminoid marshes are common along the Anisak River and on some low hills in water tracks. Alder is no longer common in this area, but open low willow communities are. These types of conditions continue eastward into the Amuik River area and to the south where broad valleys of low rolling hills occur. In general, alder is sparse and insignificant in this area, occurring on river and stream cut banks, at times following stream courses up to 500 m in elevation. Low and dwarf shrub- graminoid tussock types are more common, with willow thickets along streams and rivers or in some moist areas.

The central part of the Noatak National Preserve is composed of steep hills and rugged mountains. The area where the Noatak River cuts through is often referred to as the Grand Canyon of the Noatak River. The river course in this area occurs in a transition zone where trees are a relatively common occurrence to the west but are absent in the east. On the western end of the canyon (hills east of Kaluktavik River), white spruce (*Picea glauca*), balsam cottonwood (*Populus balsamifera*), and paper birch (*Betula papyrifera*) all occur. The paper birch was not observed in other areas in the western part of the Noatak National Preserve, although some 'tree-like' plants seemed to be a hybrid of *Betula papyrifera* and *B. glandulosa* (a shrub). The spruce and cottonwood grow in small stands or singly, whereas the birch is normally found singly. Willows are common on lower slopes and in drainages, and alder is common on steep upper slopes. In the central part of the canyon (Sisiak Creek area; fig. 7), the spruce eventually disappears. Cottonwoods are common in small groves on the river floodplain and up on the first terrace above the river (rising approximately 50 m in elevation); birch trees also are present.

West of the Sapun Creek confluence with the Noatak River, the trees disappear, and the vegetation consists primarily of tall and low shrubs along the drainages, with low and dwarf shrubs on the nearby rolling hills and lower mountain slopes (similar to figure 7

22

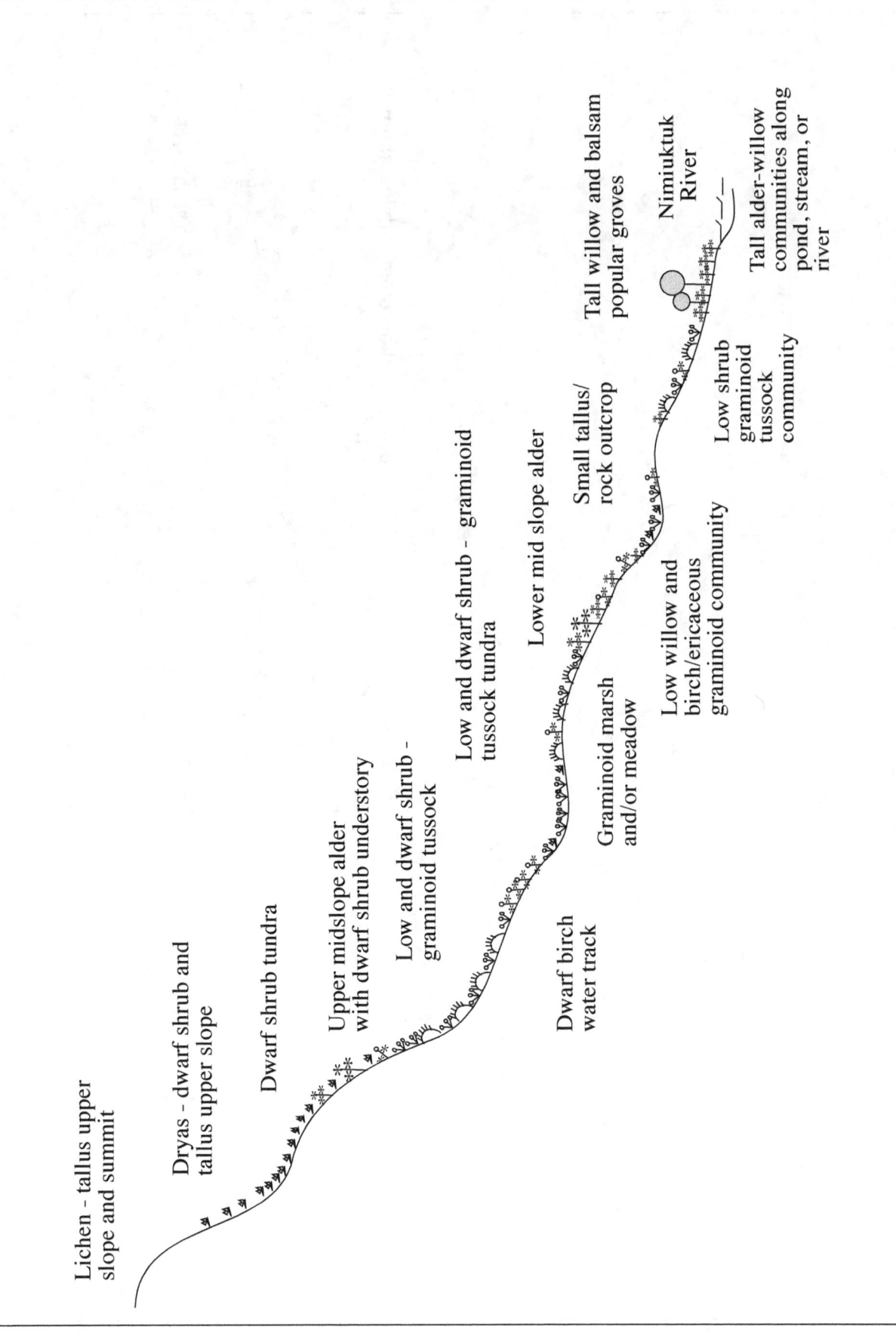

Figure 5. Typical vegetation profile of lower Nimiuktuk River valley.

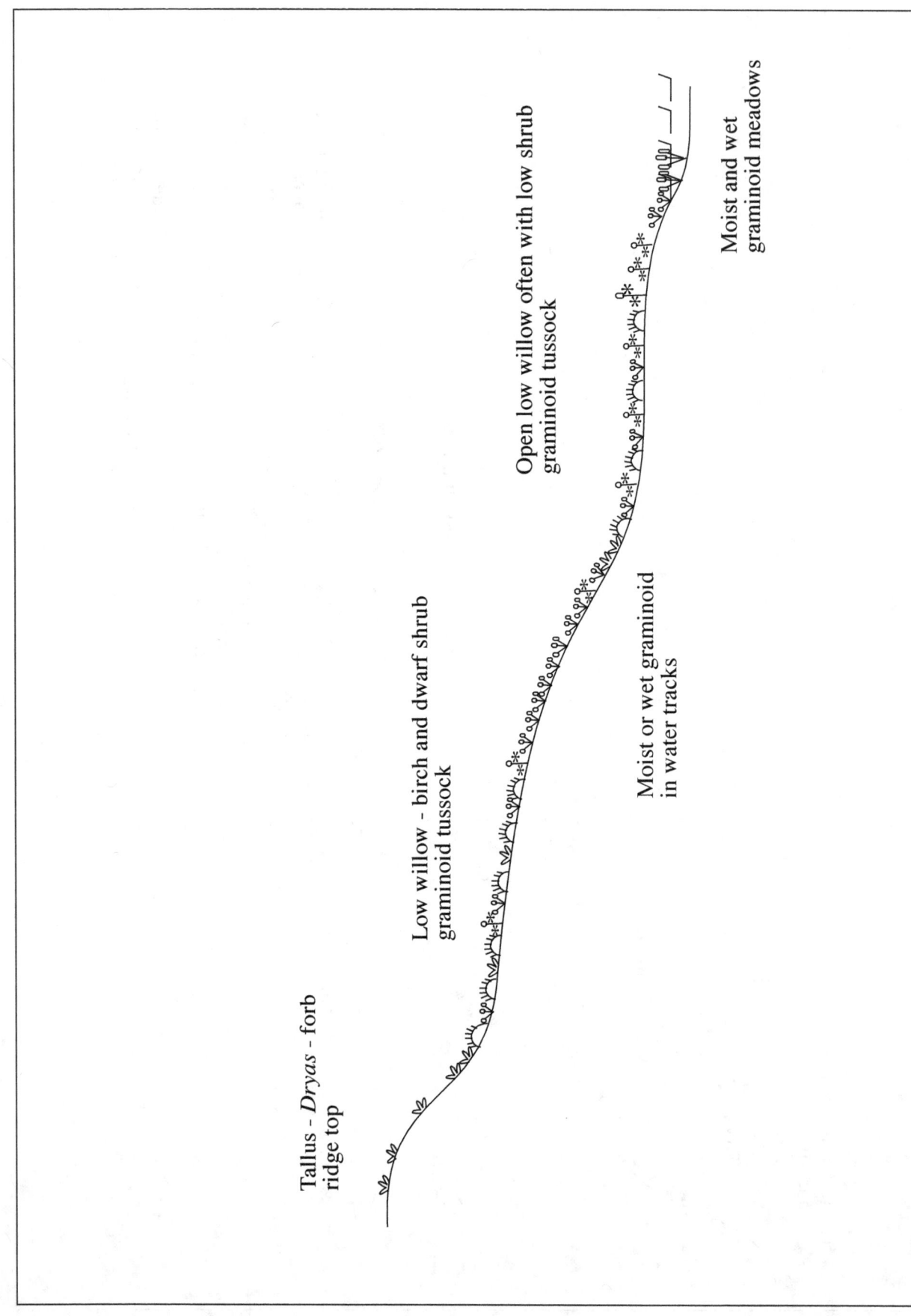

Tallus - *Dryas* - forb
ridge top

Low willow - birch and dwarf shrub
graminoid tussock

Open low willow often with low shrub
graminoid tussock

Moist or wet graminoid
in water tracks

Moist and wet
graminoid meadows

Figure 6. Vegetation profile in the Desperation Lake area of northern Noatak National Monument.

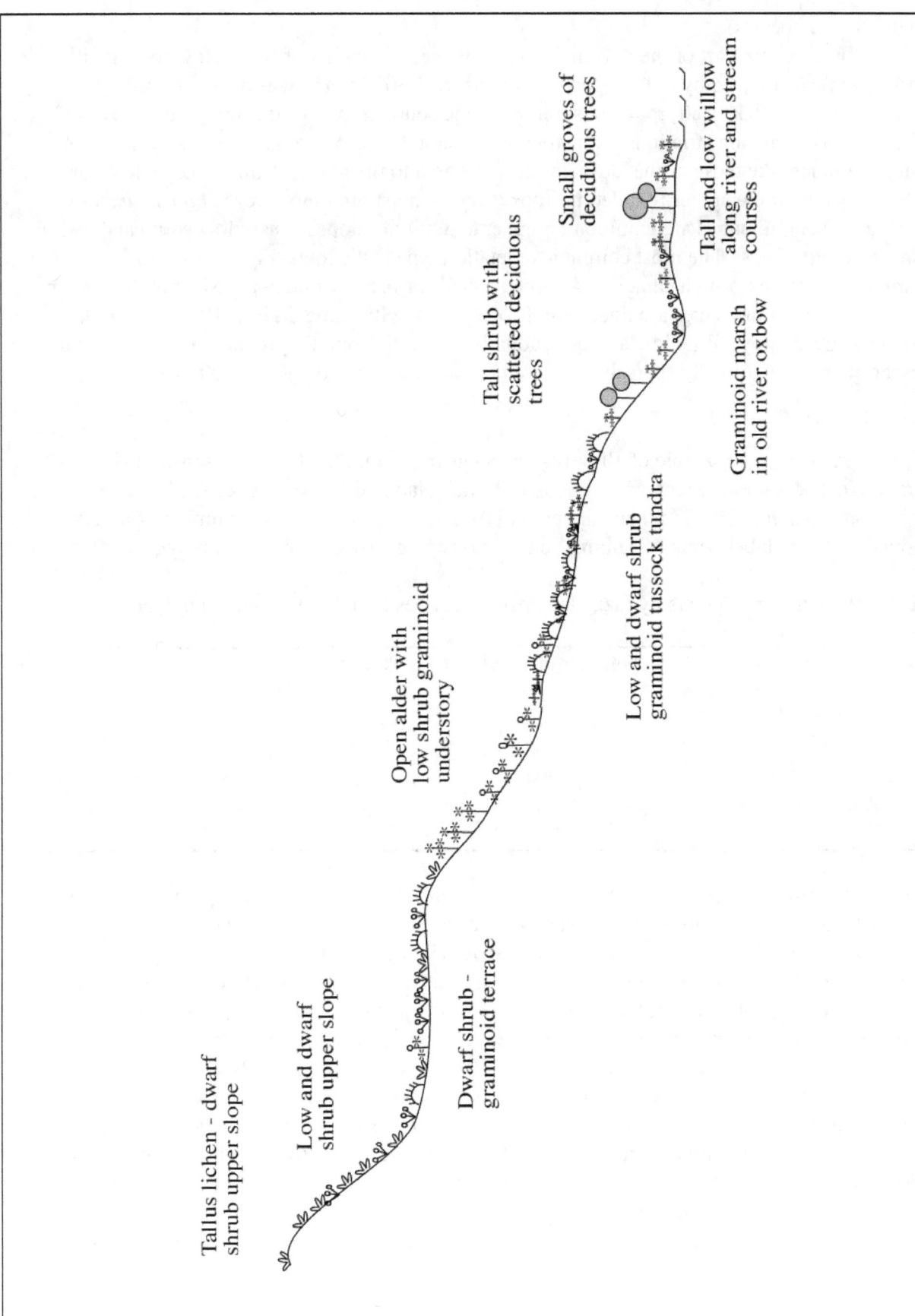

Tallus lichen - dwarf shrub upper slope

Low and dwarf shrub upper slope

Dwarf shrub - graminoid terrace

Open alder with low shrub graminoid understory

Tall shrub with scattered deciduous trees

Small groves of deciduous trees

Low and dwarf shrub graminoid tussock tundra

Graminoid marsh in old river oxbow

Tall and low willow along river and stream courses

Figure 7. Vegetation profile in the Sisiak River area along the Noatak River.

without tree species).

The eastern part of the Noatak National Preserve consists of broad, low rolling hills (to 500 m) surrounded by tall, rugged mountains (to 1,100 m) and was once covered by glacial Lake Noatak. Tall, rounded summits in the southern part of the area drained by the Coulter River contain striations indicative of old shorelines. Vegetation communities in this area are much like those of the Desperation Lake area to the north. Talus-lichen and dwarf shrubs occur on the higher rounded hilltops. Dry to moist graminoid-forb (*Equisetum* sp., *Carex* sp.) communities are common on upper and middle slopes, as are low shrub and dwarf shrub communities. The most common vegetation type is the low and dwarf shrub-graminoid tussock, which can extend uninterrupted for many kilometers. Most of the stream banks and small drainages are lined with low willows, with some high (+ 10 m) noneroded banks vegetated by tall willow and occasionally alder. Surrounding mountain summits and escarpments are normally sparsely vegetated or barren, especially above 400 m.

Map Assessment

A 10-percent sample of all polygons occurring within the Cape Krusenstern National Park, Noatak National Preserve, and Kobuk Valley National Park areas resulted in 31 polygons containing 7,158 pixels (appendix B). Table 9 shows the total number of pixels found by fuzzy label type. Assuming homogenous plant cover within each polygon and

Table 9. Number of pixels by fuzzy label for all classes found in the sample polygons

Fuzzy Label	Number of Pixels	Percent
1	434	6
2	608	8
3	1,594	22
4	2,337	33
5	2,185	31

acceptable fuzzy labels of 4 and 5, overall agreement between the mapped pixels occurring in the polygons and field observations was 64 percent. If a fuzzy label of 3 also were acceptable, then the agreement would increase to 86 percent. However, the acceptance of a fuzzy label of 3 may have more severe consequences than the acceptance of a 4 and 5. To consider a fuzzy label of 3 acceptable would depend upon the land cover class type, the ultimate use of the data, and intimate knowledge of the relationship between the class type and actual vegetation occurring in the field. Whereas the difference between a 4 and a 5 may be due to a percentage cover or height cut point, a value of 3 may represent areas that have entirely different plant species or combinations of plant species. For example, a pixel may be mapped as open low shrub- alder/willow but actually be an open low shrub-birch ericaceous. Although these two classes may be similar in terms of cover, they may be very different in terms of soils, nutrients, or wildlife use.

Table 10 provides a somewhat more detailed assessment by looking at individual

Table 10. Map assessment using weighted fuzzy labels for a 10-percent sample of the IMA polygons used during the mapping process

LCC	Description	Number Pixels	Fuzzy 5	Remaining Mismatch	Fuzzy 4	Remaining Mismatch	Fuzzy 3	Remaining Mismatch
1	Closed needleleaf forest	80	0	0	31	49	49	0
2	Open needleleaf forest	229	185	44	41	3	0	0
3	Needleleaf woodland	262	97	165	157	8	0	0
8	Tall closed alder/willow	86	19	67	57	10	0	0
9	Closed low shrub-alder/willow	543	218	325	207	118	57	61
10	Closed low shrub-birch/ericaceous	112	10	102	0	0	100	2
11	Open low shrub-alder/willow	555	98	457	206	251	1	250
12	Open low shrub-birch/ericaceous	1,104	285	819	250	569	421	148
13	Open low and dwarf shrub tussock tundra	1,431	597	834	104	730	587	143
14	Dwarf shrub tundra/dwarf shrub peatland	797	238	559	314	245	175	70
17	Open dwarf shrub-talus/lichen	201	82	119	101	18	6	12
19	Moist or dry herbaceous	981	0	0	635	346	166	180
20	Wet herbaceous	98	5	93	2	91	1	90
22	Sparsely vegetated	127	13	114	82	32	0	0
23	Barren	349	224	125	112	13	8	5
25	Clear water	182	114	68	24	44	23	21
26	Turbid water	14	0	0	7	7	0	0
27	Shadow	7	0	0	7	0	0	0
	Total	7,158	2,185	3,891	2,337	2,534	1594	982

27

Table 10. Continued

LCC	Description	Fuzzy 2	Remaining Mismatch	Fuzzy 1	Remaining Mismatch
1	Closed needleleaf forest	0	0	0	0
2	Open needleleaf forest	0	0	3	0
3	Needleleaf woodland	0	0	8	0
8	Tall closed alder/willow	0	0	10	0
9	Closed low shrub-alder/willow	17	44	44	0
10	Closed low shrub-birch/ericaceous	2	0	0	0
11	Open low shrub-alder/willow	170	80	80	0
12	Open low shrub-birch/ericaceous	63	85	85	0
13	Open low and dwarf shrub tussock tundra	143	0	0	0
14	Dwarf shrub tundra/dwarf shrub peatland	57	13	13	0
17	Open dwarf shrub-talus/lichen	10	2	2	0
19	Moist or dry herbaceous	141	39	39	0
20	Wet herbaceous	0	0	90	0
22	Sparsely vegetated	0	0	32	0
23	Barren	5	0	0	0
25	Clear water	0	0	21	0
26	Turbid water	0	0	7	0
27	Shadow	0	0	0	0
	Total	608	263	434	0

28

Table 10. Continued

LCC	Description	Number Pixels	Fuzzy 5	Remaining Mismatch	Fuzzy 4	Remaining Mismatch	Fuzzy 3	Remaining Mismatch
1	Closed needleleaf forest	80	0%	100%	39%	61%	61%	0%
2	Open needleleaf forest	229	81%	19%	18%	1%	0%	--
3	Needleleaf woodland	262	37%	63%	60%	3%	0%	--
8	Tall closed alder/willow	86	22%	78%	66%	12%	0%	12%
9	Closed low shrub-alder/willow	543	40%	60%	38%	22%	10%	11%
10	Closed low shrub-birch/ericaceous	112	9%	91%	0%	91%	89%	2%
11	Open low shrub-alder/willow	555	18%	82%	37%	45%	0%	45%
12	Open low shrub-birch/ericaceous	1,104	26%	74%	23%	52%	38%	13%
13	Open low and dwarf shrub tussock tundra	1,431	42%	58%	7%	51%	41%	10%
14	Dwarf shrub tundra/dwarf shrub peatland	797	30%	70%	39%	31%	22%	9%
17	Open dwarf shrub-talus/lichen	201	41%	59%	50%	9%	3%	--
19	Moist or dry herbaceous	981	0%	100%	65%	35%	17%	18%
20	Wet herbaceous	98	5%	95%	2%	93%	1%	92%
22	Sparsely vegetated	127	10%	90%	65%	25%	0%	25%
23	Barren	349	64%	36%	32%	4%	2%	--
25	Clear water	182	63%	37%	13%	24%	13%	12%
26	Turbid water	14	0%	100%	50%	50%	0%	50%
27	Shadow	7	0%	100%	100%	0%	0%	--
	Total	7,158	31%	69%	33%	37%	22%	15%

Table 10. Continued

LCC	Description	Fuzzy 2	Remaining Mismatch	Fuzzy 1	Remaining Mismatch
1	Closed needleleaf forest	0%	--	0%	--
2	Open needleleaf forest	0%	--	1%	--
3	Needleleaf woodland	0%	--	3%	--
8	Tall closed alder/willow	0%	12%	12%	--
9	Closed low shrub-alder/willow	3%	8%	8%	--
10	Closed low shrub-birch/ericaceous	2%	--	0%	--
11	Open low shrub-alder/willow	31%	14%	14%	--
12	Open low shrub-birch/ericaceous	6%	8%	8%	--
13	Open low and dwarf shrub tussock tundra	10%	--	0%	--
14	Dwarf shrub tundra/dwarf shrub peatland	7%	--	2%	--
17	Open dwarf shrub-talus/lichen	5%	--	1%	--
19	Moist or dry herbaceous	14%	4%	4%	--
20	Wet herbaceous	0%	92%	92%	--
22	Sparsely vegetated	0%	25%	25%	--
23	Barren	1%	--	0%	--
25	Clear water	0%	12%	12%	--
26	Turbid water	0%	50%	50%	--
27	Shadow	0%	--	0%	--
	Total	8%	6%	6%	--

classes. All map classes are represented, although some only minimally. The fuzzy columns represent the number of pixels found for each respective class that received that fuzzy value. The "Remaining Mismatch" column represents the remainder of pixels that received a fuzzy value less than the preceding higher fuzzy value. Successive mismatch columns are reduced by the sum of previous fuzzy column amounts. For example, for land cover closed low shrub-alder/willow (class 9), the "Remaining Mismatch" column following "Fuzzy 4" represents the sum of all pixels in the class (543) minus the number of pixels with a fuzzy value of 5 (218), minus the number of pixels with a fuzzy value of 4 (207). Thus, class 9 had an accuracy of approximately 78 percent (lower half of table 10) if fuzzy values of 4 and 5 were acceptable.

Using fuzzy values of 4 and 5, the four classes that had the highest agreement with the polygon data were open needleleaf forest (class 2, 99 percent), needleleaf woodland (class 3, 97 percent), open dwarf shrub-talus/lichen (class 17, 91 percent), and barren (class 23, 96 percent). Those with the worst agreement were wet herbaceous (class 20, 7 percent), followed by closed low shrub-birch/ericaceous (class 10, 8 percent).

DISCUSSION

The northwest areas land cover map was derived using parts of nine different satellite scenes, over a wide range of seasonal dates (30 June to 8 August), and using field data collected by different crews. This caused major problems in mapping such an extensive area, including unresolved classes at scene boundaries, spectral class overlap, and inconsistency in field data collection.

Differences in vegetation phenology and natural disturbances alter the way data are recorded by the sensor, making seamless data merging between satellite scenes difficult. In northwest Alaska, changes in vegetation cover across the landscape can be subtle, and slight changes in data acquisition dates may make a difference in how a particular spectral class is ultimately labeled. Early data acquisition dates (that is, June) may capture shrub vegetation in its initial leaf-out condition, thereby allowing dead, previous-year understory vegetation to show. In contrast, data acquired in July will pick up full shrub leaf-out conditions. Thus, the same vegetation community will have two very different spectral responses and may ultimately be assigned to different land cover classes. This is especially true in the Noatak National Preserve and in the central and northern parts of the Cape Krusenstern National Monument. Small changes in shrub and graminoid cover can occur within 30 to 120 m (1-4 pixels), depending on soil moisture, slope, and aspect (all of which affect the type of spectral class being identified). As an example, alder was fairly common throughout the area, although it was found most often on steeper hillslopes or mid-slopes of mountains. In many cases, the spectral class of open alderstands would be the same as those of open low shrub-dwarf birch/ericaceous cover because the understory vegetation would be dominated by dwarf birch and ericaceous plants. Alder also occurred on aspects away from the dominant sun angle (effects of shading), producing a spectral signature close to that of a dwarf birch/ericaceous type.

These types of problems can be somewhat expected, as a spectral classification is basically the grouping of spectral responses into abstract classes of shared characteristics (Norwine and Greegor, 1983). To alleviate this problem, good field information is needed for the areas in question, but was lacking in parts of this study because field information was not always collected near the time of satellite data acquisition.

Another difficulty of this mapping project was the use of three different crews to collect the *in situ* field information over a period of 4 years (1988-91). As a result, some of the field calls by different individuals were not consistent across the project area. In addition, the aerial photographs used for spectral class identification that accompanied the field data span a period of 8 years (1977-85) and predate the satellite data. Although this is not a major problem, some of the photographs showed fire scars that were completely revegetated on the satellite images. Burned areas were not visited during the field campaigns, and assumptions had to be made as to what land cover type was identified by the satellite data. Also, field data were collected for the identification and description of mapped classes and not necessarily for accuracy assessments, thereby prompting the use of "fuzzy labels" and the polygon data.

The vegetation descriptions in appendix A are broad in scope and often meager in detail. This is primarily because (1) field data collection focused on general vegetative cover instead of detailed species descriptions and (2) very little time was allowed for botanical data collection. Also, field data procedures stressed that dominant species or microcommunity (for example, tussock) cover add up to 100 percent in an effort to catagorize what the satellite sensor would detect. This left out the opportunity to record other (possibly important) species and site conditions that may have been present. It would be useful to obtain more complete species information in the future for each of the vegetation types listed to better relate how cover types change throughout the management area.

There was a problem with comparable resolution between data sets. The Landsat TM data have a pixel resolution of 30 meters, making these data very useful for landscape-scale projects (1:60,000 to 1:100,000). However, the digital elevation data, an important component for separating mixed classes and its derivatives, slope and aspect, were derived from data with an initial pixel resolution of 90 to 100 meters. This resulted in much broader changes in spectral and land cover class discrimination than desired. For example, valleys that could be identified on the Landsat data and contained classes to be modified would disappear after application of the elevation data. This also was a problem, albeit to a lesser degree, with the bedrock geology data (1:2,500,000 scale) and soils data (1:1,000,000-scale). Similar problems can occur when using winter Landsat MSS data with a nominal pixel resolution of 80 meters, but appeared to be minimal when used for conifer stratification in this study.

Map accuracies are an important result of any mapping project. They allow users to judge the usefulness of individual classes and the map as a whole. The accuracy of the final land cover from this project was lower (64 percent) than what is normally considered acceptable (80 percent or greater). The low accuracy is partially due to the use of pixel labels that occurred within the sampled polygons, a procedure that is not entirely valid but is used elsewhere and is perhaps the only logical means of obtaining a sense of the map's usefulness. Even though the polygons appeared to be homogeneous on the photograph, the influences of subtle vegetation changes across the polygon, in combination with aspect and slope effects on lighting, often lead to individual pixels being classed differently. Also, the collection of field data within those polygons was not designed to be used in an accuracy assessment. Only a small part of each polygon was visited (not the entire polygon), with the assumption that the entire polygon was characterized by the site visited. Therefore, it is not known what vegetation actually occurred within any given pixel in any given polygon.

The use of this project's accuracy assessment information is further compounded in that the sampled polygons may have been used for spectral class identification. Although some believe that, ultimately, this should make no difference on the final accuracy (Mike Fleming, USGS, oral commun.), others believe that it may and that the two data sets should be kept separate. For this type of accuracy assessment to be valid in the future, polygons used for the accuracy assessment should be kept independent of spectral class identification, and each pixel within the sample polygon should be sampled.

CONCLUSIONS

Federal land management agencies in Alaska have been using Landsat data for mapping land cover since the early to mid-1970's (Markon, 1995), the National Park Service being one of the initial users of the data (Dean and Heebner, 1982). This most recent land cover map and the resulting digital data base produced for the National Park Service's Northwest Management Area provides information that can be used by regional and local resource planners, managers, and researchers. Although many management personnel prefer higher resolution data products than the Landsat TM provides, it is currently the most available and cost effective way to obtain land cover information for large areas such as the Northwest Alaska management area.

The final land cover map may have several different applications, depending on the user and purpose. Some users may want to use the entire map, others may only be interested in one or a few classes. Although the accuracy assessment provides some information about the usefulness of the mapped data, users may want to perform more detailed analysis of the data, especially if they are interested in individual classes. For others, however, general information may suffice. For example, a wildlife biologist may only be interested in locating areas that generally contain tall and low shrub, regardless of shrub type and association with other vegetation communities. Since shrub types are generally easy to separate from nonshrub types, the current information may be sufficient.

The northwest area is a land rich in historical uses by Native Americans, containing many significant archeological sites. The land cover data base may be manipulated to show various land cover types important to animals or indigenous peoples, or it may be used in conjunction with terrain data to determine possible historical land use sites or travel routes. The fact that the data base is georeferenced also allows other data to be included for further manipulation, enhancement, or updating.

LITERATURE CITED

Ailts, B., Akkerman, D., Quirk, B., and Steinwand, D., 1990, LAS 5.0 -- An image processing system for research and production environments, *in* American Congress on Surveying and Mapping (ACSM)/American Society for Photogrammetry and Remote Sensing (ASPRS) Annual Convention, Denver, Colorado, March 1990, Proceedings: Bethesda, Md., ACSM/ASPRS, v. 4, p. 1-12.

Beikman, H.M., 1980, Geological map of Alaska: U.S. Geological Survey Map.

Coulter, H.W., Hopkins, D.M., Karlstrom, T.N.V., Pewe, T.L., Wahrahaftig, C., and
    Williams, J.R., 1965, Map showing extent of glaciation in Alaska: U.S. Geological
    Survey Miscellaneous Geologic Investigations, Map I-415, scale 1:2,500,000.

Craighead, J.J., Craighead, F.L., Craighead, D.J., and Redmond, R.L., 1988, Mapping arctic
    vegetation in northwest Alaska using Landsat MSS imagery: National Geographic
    Research, v. 4, p. 496-527

Dean, F.C., and Heebner, D.K., 1982, Landsat based vegetation mapping of Mount McKinley
    National Park region, Alaska: Alaska Cooperative Park Studies Unit, University of
    Alaska, Fairbanks.

Faeo, V., 1993, Cape Krusenstern National Monument, Alaska, satellite land cover map
    user's guide: National Park Service, Alaska Regional Office, Anchorage, Alaska, 25
    p.

Fleming, M..D., 1975, Computer-aided analysis of Landsat data: A comparison of three
    approaches including modified clustering approach: West Lafayette, Ind., Purdue
    University Laboratory for Applications of Remote Sensing, LARS Information Note
    072475, 9 p.

_____ 1988, An integrated approach for automated cover type mapping of large inaccessible
    areas in Alaska: Photogrammetric Engineering and Remote Sensing, v. 54, no. 3, p.
    357-362.

Gallant, A.L., Binnian, E.F., Omernik, J.M., and Shasby, M.B., 1995, Ecoregions of Alaska:
    U.S. Geological Survey Professional Paper 1567, 73 p.

Gopal, S., and Woodcock, C., 1994, Theory and methods for accuracy assessment of thematic
    maps using fuzzy sets: Photogrammetric Engineering and Remote Sensing, v. 60, no.
    2, p. 181-188.

Karlstrom, T.N., Coulter, H.W., Fernald, A.T., Williams, J.R., Hopkins, D.M., Pewe, T.L.,
    Drewes, H., Muller, E.H., and Condon, H., 1964, Surficial Geology of Alaska: U.S.
    Geological Survey Miscellaneous Geological Investigations Map I-357, two map
    series, scale 1:1,584,000.

Kuchler, A. W., 1966, Potential natural vegetation of Alaska: National Atlas of the United
    States of America, Washington, D.C., U.S. Geological Survey, p. 92.

Loveland, T.R., and Shaw D.M.., 1996, Multiresolution land characterization: Building
    collaborative partnerships, in Scott, J.M.., Tear, T., and Davis, F., Gap Analysis: A
    Landscape Approach to Biodiversity Planning, Proceedings of the ASPRS/GAP
    Symposium, Charlotte, N.C., National Biological Service: Moscow Idaho, p. 83-89.

Markon, C.J., 1995, History and use of remote sensing for conservation and management of
    Federal lands in Alaska, USA: Natural Areas Journal, v. 15, p. 329-338.

Markon, C.J., Fleming, M.D., and Binnian, E.F., 1995, Characteristics of vegetation
    phenology over the Alaskan landscape using AVHRR time series data: Polar Record,
    v. 31, p. 179-190.

Markon, C.J., and Wesser, S., 1997, The Bering Land Bridge National Preserve land cover
    map and its comparability with 1995 field conditions: U.S. Geological Survey Open-
    File Report, 97-103, 27 p.

Muller, S.V., Walker, D.A., Nelson, F.E., Auerback, N.A., Bockheim, J.G., Guyer, S., and Sherba, D. 1998, Accuracy assessment of a land-cover map of the Kuparuk River Basin, Alaska: considerations for remote regions: Photogrammetric Engineering and Remote Sensing, v. 64, p. 619-628.

Norwine, J. and Greegor, D.H., 1983, Vegetation classification based on advanced very high resolution radiometer (AVHRR) satellite imagery: Remote Sensing of Environment, 13, p. 69-87.

Rieger, S., Schoephorster, D.B., and Furbush, C.E., 1979, Exploratory soil survey of Alask:, U.S. Dept of Agriculture, Soil Conservation Service, 213 p.

Selkregg, L.L., 1975, Alaska regional profiles, northwest region: Anchorage, Alaska, University of Alaska, Arctic Environmental Information and Data Center, 265 p.

Soil Conservation Service, 1985, Range survey of the Seward Peninsula reindeer ranges, Alaska:. U.S. Dept. of Agriculture, Soil Conservation Service, Anchorage, Alaska,. 65 p.

Swain, P.H., and Davis, S.M., 1978, Remote sensing: the quantitative approach: McGraw Hill, Inc., New York, N.Y., 396 p.

Talbot, S.S., Fleming, M..D., and Markon, C.J., 1986, Intermediate-scale vegetation mapping in Kanuti National Wildlife Refuge, Alaska using Landsat MSS digital data: The American Society for Photogrammetry and Remote Sensing and The American Congress on Surveying and Mapping, Fall 1986, Proceedings, p. 392-406.

Talbot, S.S. and Markon, C.J., 1988, Intermediate-scale vegetation mapping of Innoko National Wildlife Refuge, Alaska , using Landsat MSS digital data: Photogrammetric Engineering and Remote Sensing, v. 54, no. 3, p. 377-383.

U.S. Congress, 1980, Alaska National Interest Lands Conservation Act (ANILCA), Public Law 96-487: Washington, D.C.

Viereck, L.A., Dyrness, C.T., Batten, A.R., and Wenzlick, K.J., 1992, The Alaska vegetation classification: U.S. Forest Service, Pacific Northwest Research Station, General Technical Report PNW-GTR-286, 278 p.

Vogelmann, J.E., Sohl, T., Campbell, P.V., and. Shaw, D.M., 1998, Regional land cover characterization using Landsat thematic mapper data and ancillary data sources: Proceedings of the 3d EMAP Symposium, April 8-11, 1997, Albany, N.Y., Environmental Monitoring and Assessment.

Vogelmann, J.E., Sohl, T., and Howard, S.M., 1998, Regional characterization of land cover using multiple sources of data: Photogrammetric Engineering and Remote Sensing v. 64, p. 45-57.

Wesser, S., 1994, A design for assessing land cover map accuracy in large and remote areas: Proceedings, 3d Circumpolar Symposium on Remote Sensing of Arctic Environments, University of Alaska, Fairbanks, Alaska, p. 50.

APPENDIX A
Class Descriptions for
the Northwest Areas Management Area
Land Cover Map

Closed Needleleaf (class 1)

Closed needleleaf forests are dominated by white spruce (*Picea glauca*) on well-drained sites and along drainages, or black spruce (*Picea mariana*) on lowland sites in the Kobuk Valley National Park. Crown closure follows that of Viereck and others (1992)[3] at 60 to 100 percent. Understory layers may consist of *Alnus* sp., *Salix* sp., *Betula glandulosa*, *Spirea beauverdiana*, *Ledum palustre*, *Arctostaphylos uva-ursi*, *Vaccinium uliginosum*, and various species of moss (particularly of the genus *Sphagnum*). Forbs and gramminoids may include *Pyrola* sp., *Equisetum silvaticum*, *E. arvense*, *Lupine* sp. *Aster* sp., *Calamagrostis canadensis*, and *Carex* sp. Mosses may include *Sphagnum* sp. and *Hylocomium* sp.

Viereck[3] classes: IA1j, IA1k, IA1l

Open Needleleaf Forest (class 2)

This class is similar to the closed needleleaf forest with the major difference being that crown closure is 25 to 59 percent. Understory vegetation is also similar, except that other ericaceous plants may be found (such as *Empetrum nigrum*), as well as numerous forbs. In some areas, lichens also are prominent.

Viereck classes: IA2e, IA2f, IA2g

Needleleaf Woodland (class 3)

Needleleaf woodland extends the conifer forest continuum to a more sparse cover with 10- to 24- percent crown closure. Species mix is similar to the class above, with a higher cover of shrubs in the understory. In the lower part of the Kobuk Valley National Park, the understory may be dominated by lichens and have few shrub or forb species present. In lowland areas, this type also may include *Betula. nana*, *Petasites frigidus*, *Empetrum nigrum*, *Rubus chamaemorus*, *Vaccinium vitis-idaea*, and *Carex bigelowii*, to name a few.

Viereck classes: IA3c, IA3d, IA3e

---

[3]Viereck, L.A., Dyrness, C.T., Batten, A.R., and Wenzlick, K.J., 1992, The Alaska Vegetation Classification: U.S. Forest Service, Pacific Northwest Research Station, General Technical Report, PNW-GTR-286, Portland, Oregon, 278 p.

Tall Open and Closed Alder/Willow (class 8)

This type occurs primarily on upper hill slopes, mid-mountain slopes, or along rivers, streams, and small drainages. Shrub canopy is greater than 75 percent, with heights at or exceeding 1.5 m. Alders (*Alnus* sp.) are more common on upper slopes or along small drainages; willows (*Salix alaxensis, S. planifolia.*) are more ubiquitous in this class. Understory vegetation may consist of graminoids (*Carex* sp., *Calamagrostis canadensis*), forbs (*Petasites* sp., *Epilobium angustifolium*), and mosses, depending on canopy closure. This type also may represent sites that contain an open tall alder/willow component but have a high understory cover of low willow (*Salix* sp.) and low or dwarf birch (*Betula glandulosa* or *B. nana*). In addition to having the traditional shrub species, this type may also include small stands or clumps of trees (*B. papyrifera* and *Populus balsamifera*) that were too small to map, or were too similar spectrally to nearby alders and willow to be described.

Viereck classes: IB1c, IB1d, IB2a, IB2b, IB2c, IIB1a, IIB1b, IIB1c, IIB1d, IIB2a, IIB2b, IIB2dIIB2e

Closed Low Shrub-Alder/Willow (class 9)

This class is often found on well-drained sites, such as stream and river banks, lake shores, and south-facing slopes. It is dominated by either alder (*Alnus* sp.) or willow (*Salix* sp.), with more than 75-percent cover that is 20 to 150 cm tall; on some sites, *Alnus* may obtain heights up to 2 m. Low birch (*Betula glandulosa*, or shrub birch) may occur mixed with the alder or willow, later grading into the closed low shrub-birch/ericaceous type as the permafrost thaw layer becomes shallower. Associated species may include *Vaccinium uliginosum, Potentilla fruticosa, Spiraea beauvardiana*, various forbs, grasses (*Calamagrostis canadensis*), mosses (*Sphagnum*), and lichens.

Viereck classes: IIC1b

Closed Low Shrub-Birch/Ericaceous (class 10)

This class is dominated by either low or dwarf shrub birch (*Betula glandulosa* or *B. nana*), along with other types of ericaceous plants, such as *Ledum decumbens* and *L. palustre, Vaccinium uliginosum, V. vitis idaea*, and *Empetrum nigrum*. Plant cover for the birch and other ericaceous species combined is greater than 75 percent, with heights greater than 20 cm but less than 150 cm. Associated species may include *Potentilla fruticosa, Salix* sp., various forbs, grasses, mosses, and lichens. This class is often found on upland tundra sites and hill slopes that are underlain by permafrost soils or on old beach dunes (with *Elymus arenarius*); or it may also dominate small stream banks.

Viereck classes: IIC1a, IIC1c

Open Low Shrub-Alder/Willow (class 11)

This class is similar to the closed low shrub-alder/willow classes except that alder/willow cover is less than 75 percent and is often found on southern aspects of low, rolling hills. Stands of open alder may be found on mid slopes of mountains (up to 600 m), upper slopes of rounded hills, and steep mid-slopes of hills. An under-story of *Betula* sp and ericaceous species is common. Occasionally *Equisetum* sp. And various graminoids and forbs also are present.

Viereck classes: IIC2g, IIC2h, IIC2i, IIC2k, IIC2l

Open Low Shrub-Birch/Ericaceous (class 12)

This class is similar to the closed low shrub-birch/ericaceous class except that the shrub cover is less than 75 percent. It is found on various land forms, including foot slopes of mountains, lower to upper slopes of low, rolling hills, and tundra areas of broad, low relief. Low and dwarf types of *Salix* are often present in small amounts; *Carex bigelowii* tussocks also may be found.

Viereck classes: IIC2c, IIC2d, IIC2e, IIC2f

Open Low and Dwarf Shrub Tussock Tundra (class 13)

This type is very similar to the open low shrub-birch/ericaceous, the main difference being that fewer low shrubs and a greater abundance of dwarf shrubs (less than 20 cm high) are associated with the graminoid tussocks. Shrub species are the same as other birch/ericaceous types. The graminoid tussocks may be formed by *Eriophorum vaginatum* or *Carex bigelowii*.

Viereck classes: IIC2a, IIC2b

Dwarf Shrub Tundra/Dwarf Shrub Peatland (class 14)

This shrub type is dominated primarily by shrubs less than 20 cm tall, such as dwarf birch (*Betula glandulosa* and/or *B. nana*) and dwarf ericaceous shrubs (*Cassiope tetragona*, *Arctostaphylos uva-ursi*, *Vaccinium uliginosum*, *V. vitis-idaea*, *Ledum palustre*, *Dryas integrifolia* or *D. octopetala*, *Rubus chamaemorus,* and *Salix sp*). Tundra communities are most common on upper slopes of mountains in the west or on hill and mountain slopes in the east. Peatland communities are common in low areas and also may include *Oxycoccus* sp. Mosses (primarily *Sphagnum* sp.) are common in peatland types; however, lichens (*Stereocaulon* sp., *Thamnolia* sp., and other fruiticose and crustose species) are more common in the tundra sites.

Viereck classes: IID1a, IID1b, IID2b, IId3a

Open Dwarf Shrub - Talus/Lichen (class 17)

This class consists of plants less than 20 cm high with 25 to 74 percent of the cover being dwarf shrubs and associated with talus and (or) lichen-covered talus. It is common on dry upper hill and mountain slopes or on other sites prone to windblown conditions. Various lichens (for example, *Cetraria*, *Thamnolia*, and *Stereocaulen*) are usually present in large amounts. Plant species may include *Dryas integrifolia* and *D. octopetala* on dry river terraces or ridge tops, in combination with *Empetrum nigrum*, *Betula nana*, *Vaccinium vitis-idaea*, and *Arctostaphylos uva-ursi* at the base of steep slopes, on solifluction lobes, and in areas of late snowpack. Various grasses and sedges (*Carex* sp.) also are common. Other plants present to a lesser extent may include various species of *Salix*, *Potentilla*, *Hedysarum*, *Rhododendron*, *Artemisia*, *Oxytropis*, and *Papaver*. Some hill slopes also may contain *Equisetum* sp.

Viereck classes: IID1c

Moist/Dry Herbaceous (class 19)

This type is dominated by sedges (primarily *Carex aquatilis* and *C. bigelowii*), normally with greater than 60 percent cover. Most sites will have other grass or grass-like plants (*Eriophorum* sp., *Luzula* sp., and *Juncus* sp.), as well as scattered shrubs (*Salix sp.*, *Arctostaphylos uva-ursi,* and *Dryas octopetala*) and forbs (*Valeriana capitata*, *Pedicularis* sp., and *Equisetum* sp.) In some areas, *C. bigelowii* or *E. vaginatum* will form tussocks. Mosses and lichens also may be present in varying amounts in the understory.

These sites can occur on a variety of sites and slopes; however, they are commonly found on well-drained hill slopes that have been burned, and in low, broad basins, and on coastal plain tundras. Site moisture is subjective, but there is not standing water. However, some sites will have standing water throughout the spring thaw, but will become dryer as the summer progresses.

Viereck classes: IIIA1a, IIIA2a, IIIA2d, IIIA2h, IIIA2i

Wet Herbaceous (class 20)

Wet herbaceous is similar to the moist/dry herbaceous class in species composition but may also contain *Arctophila fulva*, depending on location. *Hippuris vulgaris and Potentilla palustris* may be present in limited amounts. This class is found primarily in low basins and on coastal plain tundra areas where water has been impounded. The chief difference between the wet herbaceous class and the previous class is that there is standing water at the wet sites throughout the growing season.

Viereck classes: IIIA3a, IIIA3c, IIIA3f

Sparse Vegetation (class 22)

Areas that have more than 5 percent but less than 25 percent, vascular plant cover are mapped as sparse vegetation. Sites may include mountain or ridge tops, rounded or steep talus slopes, or fluvial gravel and sand bars. Vascular plants present in mountainous areas may include *Silene acaulis*, *Diapensia* sp., *Cassiope tetragona*, *Rhododendron camtschaticum*, *Vaccinium uliginosum*, *Salix* sp., *Dryas octopetala*, *Arctostaphylos rubra*, and *Oxytropis* sp. Fluvial areas may contain *Epilobium angustifolium*, *Dryas integrifolia*, *D. drummondii*, and species of *Draba* and *Carex*. Crustose and fruitocose lichens (*Cladina* sp., *Cladonia* sp.) may be present in the mountainous areas and on talus slopes as small patches with greater than 25- percent cover, but the area as a whole would still be considered sparse vegetation.

Viereck classes: None

Barren (class 23)

Barren areas consist primarily of sand, gravel, rocks, and boulders of various sizes and are often associated with active floodplains, hill summits, and mountaintops. Vascular plant cover is normally less than 5 percent; however, varying amounts of crustose lichens may be found.

Viereck classes: None

Snow/Ice/Cloud (class 24)

This type was minimal in the project area, consisting primarily of lingering snow patches in the mountains.

Viereck classes: None

Clear Water (class 25)

This class includes lakes, ponds, rivers, and offshore water bodies with little to no particulate matter.

Viereck classes: None

Turbid Water (class 26)

Turbid water comprises lakes, ponds, rivers, and offshore waters that have high particulate matter.

Viereck classes: None

<u>Shadow</u> (class 27)

The shadow class represents those areas obscured from the sensor by mountainous terrain (for example, steep north-facing slopes). Vegetation may or may not occur in these areas, depending on a combination of slope, aspect, and elevation. This class also includes those areas that are indicated as shadow because the resolution of the digital elevation data used to modify some spectral classes was more coarse than the Landsat data (see discussion section).

Viereck classes: None

APPENDIX B

Polygon information used for assessment of final map classes from Noatak National Monument

Polygon ID	LCC	Number of Pixels	Fuzzy Label	Polygon ID	LCC	Number of Pixels	Fuzzy Label
2007	9	1	1	12003	13	7	3
2007	11	47	2	12003	14	23	3
2007	12	17	5	12003	17	101	4
2007	13	50	5	12003	19	9	1
2007	14	128	4	12003	23	1	4
2007	19	31	4	13005	11	9	1
2007	20	1	3	13005	12	16	1
2022	8	2	5	13005	13	6	2
2022	11	126	4	13005	14	44	2
2022	12	15	3	13005	17	60	5
2022	13	20	3	13005	19	93	2
2022	19	1	3	13005	22	5	4
4008	11	1	1	13005	23	4	4
4008	12	17	3	15001	9	13	5
4008	13	61	3	15001	10	2	5
4008	14	2	1	15001	11	47	5
4008	19	10	4	15001	12	25	4
4008	20	1	5	15001	13	15	4
7010	8	3	1	15001	14	1	4
7010	11	4	1	15001	20	2	4
7010	14	5	1	15001	25	23	4
7010	17	6	3	15001	26	7	4
7010	19	48	2	15003	9	10	4
7010	22	10	5	15003	13	121	5
7010	23	15	4	15003	14	4	4
10002	2	3	1	15003	19	7	4
10002	3	4	1	15005	9	7	1
10002	8	1	1	15005	11	16	2
10002	9	36	1	15005	12	24	3
10002	11	66	1	15005	13	107	5
10002	12	69	1	15005	14	1	2
10002	13	16	3	15005	19	275	4
10002	14	4	1	15005	25	1	1
10002	19	1	4	15005	26	7	1
10002	20	1	5	17007	11	2	4

LCC refers to the different land cover classes shown in Table 4.

Polygon information used for assessment of final map classes
from Noatak National Monument - continuned

Polygon ID	LCC	Number of Pixels	Fuzzy Label	Polygon ID	LCC	Number of Pixels	Fuzzy Label
17007	12	36	4	24011	12	13	4
17007	13	319	3	24011	13	74	4
17007	14	172	4	24011	14	2	1
17007	19	50	4	24011	19	81	4
17013	8	9	5	25009	11	15	2
17013	9	29	5	25009	12	63	2
17013	13	4	2	25009	13	24	2
17013	17	8	2	25009	14	85	5
17013	23	4	2	25009	19	1	3
17013	25	23	3	25009	22	17	4
24006	11	1	3	25009	23	7	4
24006	12	57	3	25013	14	79	3
24006	13	158	5	25013	22	11	4
24006	19	37	4	25013	23	73	4
24011	11	3	5				

Polygon information used for assessment of final map classes from Cape Krusenstern National Preserve

Polygon ID	LCC	Number of Pixels	Fuzzy Label
1001	12	2	5
1001	13	23	5
1001	19	115	4
1001	20	3	5
2007	8	6	1
2007	10	100	3
2007	12	266	5
2007	13	13	5
2007	19	3	3
2007	20	3	1
7005	13	18	2
7005	14	153	5
7005	19	4	1
7005	22	29	1
7005	23	224	5
8002	8	8	5
8002	10	2	5
8002	11	44	5
8002	12	43	3
8002	13	30	3
8002	14	32	3
8002	17	22	5
8002	19	23	1
8002	20	41	1
8002	22	3	5
8002	25	114	5
13006	9	172	5
13006	10	6	5
13006	11	2	5
13006	12	51	4
13006	13	26	2
13006	14	5	2
13006	17	2	1
13006	19	8	3
13006	20	22	1
13006	25	1	4
14007	2	3	4
14007	3	5	4
14007	8	9	4
14007	9	39	4
14007	11	29	4
14007	12	26	4
14007	13	15	4
14007	19	28	4
14007	20	24	1
14007	23	8	3
14007	25	20	1

Polygon information used for assessment of final map classes
from Kobuk National Park

Polygon ID	LCC	Number of Pixels	Fuzzy Label	Polygon ID	LCC	Number of Pixels	Fuzzy Label
23	2	6	5	46	8	5	4
23	3	43	4	46	9	24	4
23	8	43	4	46	13	60	2
23	9	17	2	75	11	85	2
23	11	3	2	75	12	56	4
23	14	3	2	75	13	125	5
25	2	12	4	75	14	17	3
25	3	97	5	75	19	88	3
25	9	57	3	77	11	2	5
25	11	16	4	77	12	43	4
25	12	1	3	77	13	97	3
36	1	46	3	77	14	9	4
36	2	26	4	77	19	3	1
36	9	2	4	122	3	4	1
36	11	4	2	122	9	132	4
36	13	4	2	122	13	23	3
36	14	1	2	127	10	2	2
36	17	2	2	127	12	256	3
36	19	65	3	127	22	49	4
42	1	31	4	127	23	12	4
42	2	159	5	127	27	1	4
42	3	52	4	149	9	4	5
42	13	1	2	149	11	33	4
42	14	3	2	149	12	8	3
42	23	1	2	149	13	14	3
46	1	3	3	149	14	24	3
46	2	20	5	149	22	3	1
46	3	57	4	149	27	6	4

www.ingramcontent.com/pod-product-compliance
Lightning Source LLC
Chambersburg PA
CBHW080922290526
45795CB00007BA/2624

9781492701231